JOURNEY ON THE FORBIDDEN PATH:
CHRONICLES OF A DIPLOMATIC MISSION TO THE ALLEGHENY COUNTRY,
MARCH - SEPTEMBER, 1760

Journal

of Mr Christⁿ Fred Post, in Company with Teedyuscung, Mr John Hays, Isaac Still, & Moses Tattamy, to the great Council of the different Indian Nations, 1760.

April 1st Return'd to Philadelphia, being somewhat recovered from the Dangerous Accident I met with on my Way to New York.

22^d I received my Instructions from his Honour the Governor. Afterwards I visited Mr Logan & Colonel Boquet, with whom I conferred about preparing a Writing to his Excellency General Amhirst, concerning his Message to the Indians.

23^d I spoke with the Commissioners, by whom it was agreed on, that Moses Tattamy should go alone to Teedyuscung to acquaint him of the Misfortune that had befallen me, & that Isaac Still sh^d wait for the Generals Answer. To my surprise, Moses Tattamy & Isaac Still both came to take leave of me, to go to Teedyuscung; which troubled me, as I feared it wo'd be attended with bad Consequences, Nevertheless I deliver'd them the Message & String of Wampum from the Governor.

29th I was sent for to the Governor; from whom I had the Honour to receive the agreeable Answer & Message from his Excellency General Amhirst, that had been

settled

Journal of Mr. Christn. Fred Post, in Company with Teedyuscung, Mr. John Hays,
Isaac Still & Moses Tattamy, to the great Council of the different Indian Nations,
1760. First page. In the collections of the Historical Society of Pennsylvania, Am-12605

Transactions
of the
American Philosophical Society
Held at Philadelphia
For Promoting Useful Knowledge
Volume 89, Pt. 2

JOURNEY ON THE FORBIDDEN PATH:
CHRONICLES OF A DIPLOMATIC MISSION TO THE ALLEGHENY COUNTRY, MARCH - SEPTEMBER, 1760

EDITED BY
Robert S. Grumet

WITH TRANSLATIONS OF DELAWARE WORDS BY
James A. Rementer
and
Bruce L. Pearson

AMERICAN PHILOSOPHICAL SOCIETY
INDEPENDENCE SQUARE • PHILADELPHIA
1999

ISBN:0-87169-892-7
US ISSN: 0065-9746

Library of Congress Cataloging-in-Publication Data

Journey on the forbidden path : chronicles of a diplomatic mission to
    the Allegheny country, March-September, 1760 / edited by Robert S.
    Grumet ; with translations of Delaware words by James A. Rementer.
        p.   cm. -- (Transactions of the American Philosophical
    Society, ISSN 0065-9746 ; v. 89, pt. 2)
    Includes expedition journals of Christian Frederick Post and John
    Hays.
    Includes bibliographical references (p.   ) and index.
    ISBN 0-87169-892-7
    1. Pennsylvania--History--French and Indian War, 1755-1763-
    -Sources. 2. United States--History--French and Indian War,
    1755-1763--Sources. 3. Delaware Indians--History--18th century-
    -Sources. 4. Indians of North America--Pennsylvania--History--18th
    century--Sources. 5. Post, Christian Frederick, 1710?-1785-
    -Manuscripts. 6. Hays, John, 1729 or 30-1796--Manuscripts.
    I. Post, Christian Frederick, 1710?-1785. II. Hays, John, 1729 or
    30-1796. III. Grumet, Robert Steven. IV. Series.
    E199.J928 1999
    973.2'6--dc21
                                                            99-13908
                                                                 CIP

In Memory of William A. Hunter

.

CONTENTS

ACKNOWLEDGMENTS

William A. Hunter worked on the manuscript for several years, obtaining new translations of Delaware words from Eastern Oklahoma Delaware traditionalist Nora Thompson Dean. Sadly, Hunter passed away before he could see the manuscript into print. More than another twenty years passed before James A. Rementer, a student of Delaware language and culture, submitted a copy of Hunter's manuscript for editorial consideration by the *Bulletin of the Archaeological Society of New Jersey* editor, Charles A. Bello.

Bello brought the manuscript to the editor of this publication. Review of the manuscript revealed that the Post account contained substantial amounts of new information. Development of a monograph collating the Post and Hays accounts provided a rare opportunity to contrast systematically different versions of multiple texts documenting first-hand observations made in a limited and clearly identified area over a brief span of time. Inclusion of council minutes, treaty speeches, passports, and other related documents presented an even rarer chance to present primary documents placing events associated with a particular effort in frontier diplomacy into their broader historic context.

Rementer gave permission to use the manuscript to develop this study. Working closely with the editor, he contributed new translations and provided review comments. Linguist Bruce L. Pearson provided the translation of Post's Delaware name. The Historical Society of Pennsylvania granted permission to publish the copy of the Post Journal in their collections. The editor consulted the microfilm copy of the Hays Diary on file in the Pennsylvania State Archives originally published in Hunter (1954). Contrast revealed substantial differences in the two documents. The editor accordingly prepared a new transcript from the microfilmed original. He also prepared new footnotes for the diary and all other text presented in the monograph.

The substantially expanded study exceeded the limited page limits of the *Bulletin*. Editor Bello gave his support to efforts to find another publisher. The editor subsequently submitted the work to the American Philosophical Society in Philadelphia. The manuscript was accepted for publication as a monograph in the American Philosophical Society's *Transactions* series during the fall of 1998. American Philosophical Society publications editor, Carole LeFaivre-Rochester and her staff, saw the manuscript through production. Technical assistance was provided by Harry Parker, division chief of the

Pennsylvania State Archives and Mike Sherlon, Archives associate archivist. Historical Society of Pennsylvania coordinator for rights and reproduction, Bruce Scherer, arranged for permission to publish the Post journal. Research Service division coordinator Sandra Rayser provided a timely photocopy of the manuscript. James Farrell designed the map showing the mission's route from Easton to Secaughcung.

Robert Grumet
May 1999

INTRODUCTION

THE STRUCTURE OF THE VOLUME

This volume draws together records documenting a little known diplomatic effort to establish peace along the war-torn Appalachian frontier during the spring, summer, and fall of 1760. Assembled here is a representative sample of the council minutes, speeches, letters of correspondence, warrants, inventories, passports, journals, diaries, and other types of records documenting a frontier diplomatic mission of the period. These records reveal something of the range and diversity of documentary materials available to scholars interested in reconstructing diplomatic events along a distant frontier during a critical period of American history. Individually, they document political maneuvers and details of everyday life, many of which are recorded nowhere else. Collectively, they provide additional keys to understand better how Indians and colonists shaped a new diplomatic landscape along the Pennsylvania frontier after the British succeeded in breaking French power in North America in 1760.

THE SITUATION IN 1760

Pennsylvania's residents greeted the New Year of 1760 with wary hopes for peace. War with the Delawares and other former Indian allies joining the French after Braddock's defeat in 1755 had ravaged the province's frontiers for nearly five years. Treaties with Indian nations at Easton brokered through the Eastern Delaware leader Teedyuscung beginning in 1756 had opened the way west and allowed British troops to finally secure the strategic Forks of the Ohio at present-day Pittsburgh by the fall of 1758. Other British successes in 1759 at Niagara, Ticonderoga, and, most decisively, at Quebec, sealed the doom of the French war effort in North America. Realizing that the French would almost certainly lose most of their remaining posts in Canada when the campaigning season began in the spring, Indian and British diplomats throughout the region maneuvered to reinforce spheres of influence, secure established boundaries, and erect new ones along the now fluid frontier through treaties (Jones 1982, McConnell 1992, White 1991).

Treaties were the primary vehicles used to mediate disputes dividing competing provinces, polities, interest groups, and individuals everywhere in

1

the Northeast. Colonial governors, like Pennsylvania's James Hamilton, saw treaties with powerful frontier tribes as opportunities to secure and extend provincial borders against French enemies and colonial rivals. Within each colony, contending political, religious, ethnic, and other factions pressed governors to obtain treaty terms favorable to their interests.

Eastern Indian diplomats like Teedyuscung used treaty agreements to play contending colonists off one another as they struggled to maintain precarious positions on lands claimed by the powerful Iroquois Confederacy and increasingly penetrated by settlers moving ever-westward. Farther west, Tamaqua, Shingas, and other Ohio Valley Indian leaders rejecting Iroquois authority pursued independent policies of their own. Caught in between, Christian Indian culture-brokers like Moses Tunda Tatamy, frontier diplomats like lay missionary Christian Frederick Post, Moravian Indian converts, and millenarian Munsees following the prophet Papoonan at Wyalusing struggled to survive along an increasingly restive frontier.

Provinces used land conveyances signed with Indian nations as weapons in inter-colonial boundary disputes that historian Francis Jennings has called "Deed Wars" (Jennings 1976:128-145). Pennsylvania and New York had been fighting over the upper Susquehanna lands ever since New York Governor Thomas Dongan asserted English sovereignty over lands claimed as conquered by the Iroquois in 1683 (Jennings 1984:226-30). Refusing to recognize New York's claim, Pennsylvania obtained its own Iroquois deeds to Susquehanna Valley lands below Wyoming in 1749 and 1754 (Jennings 1988:101-06, A.F.C. Wallace 1990:39). In 1755 John Henry Lydius, an agent of the newly established Connecticut-based Susquehanna Company with an unsavory reputation, made an already difficult situation even more complex. Like many colonies, Connecticut's charter bounds stretched to include all lands between the Atlantic and Pacific Ocean and its northern and southern lines of latitude. Determined to acquire title to as much land as possible within these bounds even as the specter of frontier war loomed, profit-seeking Susquehanna Company directors from over-populated Connecticut ordered Lydius to obtain Indian deeds to Susquehanna Valley territory by any means necessary. Making extravagant promises and liberally lubricating the deal with liquor, Lydius managed to get several Indians to put their marks upon two deeds conveying most of the Susquehanna Valley lands above Wyoming to the Company (Jennings 1988:106-08, A.F.C. Wallace 1990:59-66). Outraged by what they regarded as an unwarranted and illegitimate intrusion into their own land and suspecting Quaker collusion in the sale, Pennsylvania proprietary authorities threatened to evict any New Englanders moving into the area without their permission. Ignoring these warnings, New Englanders moved to the Delaware River and began preparing to penetrate the Susquehanna Valley by 1760.

Intent upon imposing imperial order over this seething melange of contending peoples, parties, and interests, Crown representatives like General Sir Jeffery Amherst, Commander-in-Chief of British forces in North America and Sir William Johnson, His Majesty's "Sole Agent and Super-intendent of the Six Nations and their Confederates," worked to implement policies formulated half a world away along a volatile and still violent frontier torn by war and divided into a seemingly kaleidoscopic array of conflicting interest groups.

DRAMATIS PERSONAE

Many of the people named above figure prominently in the documents chronicling the diplomatic maneuvers to establish a new framework for peace along the Allegheny frontier during the spring and summer of 1760. In an addendum to the first of these, a journal of the journey published here for the first time, Christian Frederick Post first mentions the impending grand Indian council to be held in the Allegheny Country. The proposed agenda included the question of peace with the British, return of prisoners, and what should be done about a recent rash of gratuitously wanton murders of peaceable Indian people in Pennsylvania by frontier vigilantes. Post had learned of the meeting from Teedyuscung, who had planned to add luster to his reputation as a major player in frontier diplomacy by attending the meeting alone as the sole representative of the Pennsylvania Indians and their colonial allies. Distrusting Teedyuscung but seeing an opportunity to further provincial interests along the frontier, Pennsylvania governor James Hamilton ordered Post to accompany the Delaware chief to the meeting. Much to Teedyuscung's chagrin, Post was not dispatched to serve as a mere travel companion. Instead, he formally was given several messages to deliver at the council and privately asked to describe conditions and the land along the route.

Post has long been regarded as a colorful if somewhat enigmatic figure in frontier history. By all accounts, he was an adventurous spirit combining a restless nature and a strong sense of devout religiosity with a surprising degree of respect for beliefs and customs of Indian people. Historian Paul A. W. Wallace wrote that he possessed three qualities required by frontier diplomats; "integrity, devotion to the job at hand, courage, and sympathy

3

with and respect for the native people among whom he worked" (P.A.W. Wallace 1958:36).

Post's career has long been relegated to brief anecdotes, incidental notices, and obscure footnotes. The only full-length treatment of his life appears in a still-unpublished doctoral dissertation (Chase 1980). Chase's research documents that Post was born in Conitz, East Prussia, sometime around 1710. He worked as a cabinet maker before joining the Moravian Church and immigrating to Bethlehem, Pennsylvania in 1742. The highly idiosyncratic spelling and halting syntax so evident in account of his conversation with Papoonan at Wyalusing on 20 May, 1760, the only document written in his hand published in this monograph, affirms that Post was a man of limited education who wrote and spoke English with less than complete assurance. Other more conventionally composed documents attributed to Post's pen were almost certainly much-edited copies made by Charles Thomson and other provincial scribes, secretaries, and amanuenses.

Evidently anxious to see the frontier as soon as possible, Post quickly persuaded church authorities to send him along with several other lay workers to the Moravian Indian mission communities in and around Shekomeko in New York's Berkshire Mountain foothills in 1743. There he married a Wampanoag woman named Rachel. Learning the Mahican language, he lived at Shekomeko until New York authorities, suspecting that the Moravian Indians were spying for the French, drove them and their missionaries away shortly after fighting between Great Britain and France brought on by King George's War spread to North America in 1745. Post and his wife moved to Bethlehem, where Rachel died in 1747.

Invited by the Mohawk leader Hendrick, Post and a young 24-year-old missionary named David Zeisberger moved to Canajoharie to learn the Mohawk language in 1745. Arrested by New York authorities, Post was imprisoned for seven weeks. Returning to Bethlehem after his release, he served as a frontier scout safeguarding the security of the Moravian missions among the Delawares and other exiled tribes along the Lehigh and Susquehanna valleys. Around this time the Delawares gave Post the name *Wallangundowngen* (Hazard, ed.1852a [8]:690). Linguist Bruce L. Pearson translates the name as *Wdangundawakan*, "making a good blessing," the Delaware expression for peace. In 1749, Post married Agnes, a Delaware convert and daughter-in-law of Teedyuscung, who by then had become an influential Wyoming Valley Delaware leader.

Post left Pennsylvania shortly after her death in 1751 to join an abortive effort to establish a Moravian mission in Labrador. Returning to Wyoming the following year, he tried to prevent Teedyuscung and other Eastern Delawares from establishing an alliance with the French. Post's efforts failed. Angered by the loss of his people's lands and infuriated by Six Nations' collusion in their dispossession, Teedyuscung led Delaware warriors against the British following Braddock's defeat in 1755. Realizing that his life would be in danger in Wyoming, Post moved back to Bethlehem.

Post served as a messenger and scout as Delaware and other Indian warriors raided the Pennsylvania borderlands during the three years following Braddock's defeat. When he learned that Susquehanna Delawares finally weary of the war were receptive to peace proposals, he arranged for Pennsylvania authorities to dispatch him and a young assistant named Charles Thomson to meet with Teedyuscung and the other chiefs at Wyoming in the spring of 1758. Shortly thereafter, Post, New Jersey Christian Delaware interpreter Isaac Still, and a Pennsylvania militia officer named John Hays accompanied Teedyuscung on two diplomatic missions to major councils held by the Western Delawares and their Shawnee, Wyandot, and other allies in the Ohio Valley. Post's often-cited journals of these western trips remain the best-known publications documenting his career as a frontier diplomat (Post 1904).

Supported by Teedyuscung, Post helped to convince the assembled nations to abandon their French alliance. This cleared the way for a British expedition to take finally the strategic Forks of the Ohio at present-day Pittsburgh in late 1758. In early 1760, both men prepared to return to the Ohio Valley, Post to represent Pennsylvanian interests and obtain the release of unredeemed captives prisoners and Teedyuscung to revive his waning influence among the Western Delawares.

Provincial authorities selected Hays to again accompany Post as a bodyguard on this expedition. Little is known about the man whose journal and diary of the journey follows Post's account. Son of a prominent Lehigh Valley Scotch-Irish innkeeper residing in present-day Weaversville, Pennsylvania, Hays was a 30 year old militia lieutenant when he accompanied Post on the journey to Allegheny Country.

Post's and Hays's other companion, Teedyuscung, had already emerged as a major figure in frontier diplomacy. Unlike Post, Teedyuscung has been the subject of a major biography (Wallace 1990) and a more recent article examining evidence of the earliest phase of his documented career (Becker 1992). Born somewhere near Trenton, New Jersey around 1700, he was among those Delawares forced to immigrate to the Forks of the Delaware following the loss of most of their remaining ancestral lands in central parts of the province during the 1730s. Rejecting Pennsylvanian proprietary claims to the bulk of his people's lands along the west bank of the Delaware River following the Walking Purchase of 1737, Teedyuscung was among those leaders who resisted Iroquois attempts to pressure Delawares to move farther west to lands under Six Nations authority in the Wyoming Valley. He joined the Moravian brethren at the Lehigh Valley mission at Gnadenhütten (at the mouth of the Mahoning River above the Lehigh Water Gap in present-day Lehighton, Pennsylvania) after putting his mark the earlier-mentioned 1749 deed conveying Delaware lands above the Walking Purchase bounds between the Delaware and Susquehanna rivers. Taking the name Gideon following his baptism, Teedyuscung lived with the Moravians for four years. He refused to give up efforts to reclaim his people's lands, and, ultimately unwilling to accept uncritically Moravian precepts or peaceably submit to Iroquois hegemony, Teedyuscung took up the responsibilities of a Delaware chief and moved to the Wyoming Valley in 1754.

Teedyuscung initially remained neutral as most Delawares went to war against the British during the summer of 1755. Finally compelled to avenge the uncondoled murder of several of his people by Pennsylvanian colonists, Teedyuscung joined the fight against the British. He remained on the battlefield long enough to press forcefully his people's land claims and assert their right to determine their own destiny. During the summer of 1756, Teedyuscung put out his first peace feelers to Pennsylvania. Encouraged by favorable responses to these efforts, Teedyuscung employed his considerable skills as a culture broker to begin negotiations between the warring parties. Championed by Pennsylvania Quakers anxious to use him in their ongoing struggle with proprietary interests, warily regarded by Pennsylvania authorities, and derided as a shameless opportunist and drunkard by powerful enemies like Sir William Johnson and his Iroquois associates, he succeeded in bringing the Delawares and their confederates to a series of treaties at Easton, Pennsylvania establishing a framework for peace between 1756 and 1759. He began efforts to extend diplomatic feelers to still-hostile Indian communities along the upper Susquehanna and Allegheny valleys immediately afterward.

James Hamilton represented the province of Pennsylvania at the more recent of these Easton treaty conferences. Born in Virginia in 1710, Hamilton was raised in Philadelphia and educated in law in England. Independently wealthy and a strong supporter of the proprietors, he served as a member of the provincial assembly (1734-39) and was elected mayor of

Philadelphia in 1745. First appointed lieutenant governor in 1748, he served until quarrels over several key issues of defense and finance with the Quaker-dominated assembly led to his resignation in 1754. He was reappointed to a second term in November, 1759 with instructions from the crown and the proprietors to vigorously secure and defend provincial borders and interests.

Sir William Johnson's own instructions accompanying his appointment as Superintendent of Indian Affairs for all British possessions north of the Ohio River in 1756 made him sole crown agent to the Iroquois Confederacy and their affiliates. Remembered as the most prominent frontier diplomat of his era, Johnson's life and career have been the subjects of considerable scholarly interest for many years (e.g., Flexner 1979; Hamilton 1976, Sullivan et al. 1921-65). Johnson was born into a family of Irish gentry in 1715. He came to America in 1737 and took up the position of administrator of a vast estate owned by his uncle, the prominent British admiral Sir Peter Warren, in New York's Mohawk Valley. There he established close relations with his Mohawk Indian neighbors, familiarizing himself with their language and customs. Skillfully capitalizing on these connections, Johnson amassed a considerable estate of his own from profits garnered in the fur trade and the burgeoning market in Indian real estate by the time the Seven Years War broke out in 1755.

Commissioned a major general of provincial troops, Johnson was made a baronet after defeating a French army at Lake George in 1755. Further honors followed when the king made Johnson both colonel and crown agent of the Six Nations in 1756. Preoccupied by the many demands of wartime Indian diplomacy, Johnson appointed fellow trader George Croghan deputy superintendent representing crown interests along the vulnerable Pennsylvania frontier. Together, both men worked to maintain royal authority in a region increasingly torn by factional politics, ethnic conflict, and race hatred intensified by the violent ferocity of frontier warfare.

Johnson was not the only official carrying a royal commission to conduct business on behalf of the crown in the British provinces. A career soldier named Sir Jeffery Amherst (1717-97) was appointed Commander-in-Chief of all British forces in North America in 1759. Anxious to take Montreal and thus complete the conquest of New France, Amherst supported diplomatic efforts to shore up his exposed left flank by restoring peace with the Western Indian nations by the time the campaigning season reopened in 1760, but he was unwilling to consider seriously Indian concerns or accommodate Native American sensibilities. In the speech he prepared for Post to deliver to the

Allegheny tribes. Amherst threatened retaliation against treaty-breakers while insisting on the right to build forts anywhere he chose. As Post foresaw, such peremptory rhetoric did little to ease Indian anxieties at a time when a more conciliatory approach offered the best hopes for peace and security.

THE FORBIDDEN PATH

Teedyuscung, Post, and their companions selected the Forbidden Path as the quickest and most direct route to the great Indian council. As described by P.A.W. Wallace (1965:46-48), the eastern terminus of the Forbidden Path was located at the town of Tioga (present-day Athens, Pennsylvania) where the Chemung River flowed into the North Branch of the Susquehanna. The path led up the Chemung Valley past multi-cultural expatriate Indian communities at Kanawohalla (modern Elmira, New York), Assinisink (Corning, New York), and Painted Post to Secaughcung at the headwaters of a tributary of the Chemung known as the Canisteo River. Passing across the height of land separating the Ohio, Great Lakes, and Susquehanna drainages, the path crossed the Genesee River and went on to pass through many Seneca and Mingo towns lining the upper Allegheny River.

Leading directly into the heart of the central New York Iroquois heartland, the Forbidden Path stood at a strategic transportation break linking river systems ultimately flowing into Chesapeake Bay, the Great Lakes, and the Ohio Valley. Small wonder, then, that the Unami Delaware warrior Squash Cutter warned Post and his party away on 17 June 1760 saying, "It is not allow'd either for you or our cousin [Teedyuscung] to travel it, & it is moreover dangerous, I myself must go it blindfolded." Years later, a Seneca chief challenged Moravian missionary David Zeisberger's presence on the path in 1767 asking "how comes it that you travel such an unfrequented road, which is no road for whites and on which no white man has ever come?" (Hulbert and Schwarze 1912:47).

Most people living in the Indian towns along the path visited by Teedyuscung, Post, and their party in the 1760 diplomatic mission had resided in the region for only a few years. The Chemung Valley had been virtually abandoned for a century and a half after most of its Susquehannock inhabitants moved from the headwaters of the watershed bearing their name to the lower reaches of the river (Kent 1984:14-18, 295-307). The Iroquois used the area as a virtually uninhabited hunting ground and buffer zone guarding the southern approaches to their homeland. Permanent settlements

INTRODUCTION

began to be constructed in the area when the Iroquois Council invited exiles forced from other regions to settle in the upper Susquehanna Country during the second quarter of the eighteenth century. Dispossessed Munsees, Delawares, and Mahicans moved to the region from the east. Conoys, Saponis, and Cherokees came from the south, Mesquakies came from the west, expatriate Iroquois called Mingos moved from the north, and scattered Shawnees gathered together in new communities along the Susquehanna and its tributaries.

Most of these people settled in riverbank towns situated on fertile, level, and well-drained soils at or near the mouths of major tributary streams. Survivors of more than 100 years of contact with Europeans, they utilized both old and new tools, techniques, and technologies tried and tested in demanding frontier conditions (Grumet 1995). People dressed in clothing crafted from skins and cloth decorated with colorful geometric and floral designs woven from dyed quills and imported glass beads. Hunters and warriors armed themselves with traditional bows, arrows, and clubs and imported firearms and metal knives and axes. Traditional bark-covered sapling-framed longhouses were erected alongside log cabins patterned after structures built by German and Scandinavian immigrants. Corn, beans, and squash grew in cleared cultivated fields near orchards of apple, cherry, pear, and peach trees. Menus included traditional fare from the hunter's game bag like deer, bear, and wildfowl as well as more newly adopted imports like wheat flour, coffee, tea, and the flesh of domesticated pigs, cows, and chickens.

The inhabitants of this new world lived in a culturally complex resource-rich country presenting unprecedented opportunities (Mancall 1991:27-70). Pressures exerted by Iroquois sachems and a bewildering array of colonial soldiers, diplomats, traders, and missionaries added to the day-to-day stresses of everyday life. Strangers in a strange land, many succumbed to the ravages of anomie, anger, and alcohol abuse (e.g., Hauptman 1980). Some relied upon traditional beliefs while others turned to Christianity. Increasing numbers began listening to Papoonan, Wangomend, and other prophets who started preaching nativistic millenarian doctrines in the Susquehanna Valley Indian towns (Dowd 1992:27-33). Whatever their thoughts, experiences, or philosophies, all looked on outsiders with deep suspicion and hostility. It was into this world that Teedyuscung, Post, and their party journeyed on the Forbidden Path in the spring of 1760.

THE JOURNEY

Preparations for the journey on the Forbidden Path were first put in motion when Teedyuscung arrived in Philadelphia in December, 1759. As mentioned earlier, he had come to the provincial capital with news of his invitation to a great council to be held by the Western Indians in Ohio Country during the coming spring. As eager to protect his province's proprietary interests in the Ohio lands against the claims of Virginia, New York, and Connecticut rivals as he was for peace on the frontier, newly appointed Pennsylvania lieutenant governor James Hamilton quickly moved to assure that his province's interests were represented at the council. Hamilton's swift response may have been prompted by reports that prospective council participants were looking for ways to stop most effectively further colonial expansion into their lands.

Several official messages to the Indians were prepared, each accompanied by appropriate wampum belts and strings. Hamilton's message particularly emphasized restoration of peace and return of captives, many of whom had been held prisoner for nearly five years. Amherst's message, by contrast, offered protection to friends, promised retribution to enemies, and demanded acceptance of British forts on Indian land.

Hamilton and his council appointed Teedyuscung as special envoy of the province. Moravian lay minister Christian Frederick Post, then a 50-year-old forest diplomat with nearly 20 years of experience under his belt, and 30-year-old John Hays were appointed to accompany the Delaware diplomat. Officially designated as Teedyuscung's advisor, Post was instructed to invite the Western Indians to come to a council in Philadelphia later that summer. Hays was to serve as Post's companion and bodyguard. Hamilton further arranged for two Christian Delawares named Moses Tunda Tatamy and Isaac Still to accompany the party as intermediaries and interpreters.

Tatamy was one of the very few Delaware Indians allowed to remain in the Forks of the Delaware above Easton after Iroquois diplomat Canastego ordered them to abandon lands lost in the 1737 Walking Purchase at a conference held in Philadelphia in 1742 (Hunter 1996). Given a deed to 300 acres of land in the present Northampton county village bearing his name, Tatamy was baptized by Presbyterian missionary David Brainerd three years later.

Both Tatamy and Isaac Still were bilingual speakers of Delaware and English familiar with the customs and politics of people living on both sides of the frontier. Still belonged to a family of Delawares who chose to return to

New Jersey rather than take their chances farther west. He was literate and, if the large print used in the messages especially written for him to deliver is any indication, evidently near-sighted as well.

Teedyuscung returned to his home in the Wyoming Valley shortly after departing from Philadelphia. Post left the city in company with Teedyuscung's son, Captain Bull, and another Delaware named Joseph Peepy on 3 May, 1760. Tatamy and Still had gone on ahead. Joining up with Hays at his father's tavern in Weaversville on May 8, the party arrived at Teedyuscung's town at Wyoming on the North Branch of the Susquehanna River near present-day Wilkes-Barre on May 11. Joined by Tatamy, Still, and Teedyuscung, the party, now numbering 14, began traveling upriver on May 16. They stopped at the Indian town of Wyalusing to speak with the Munsee prophet Papoonan on May 20. Pressing on, the party arrived at the mouth of the Chemung River at Tioga on May 22.

From Tioga, the party turned up the Chemung River to follow the Forbidden Path. The path passed through one of the last portions of the region largely uncharted by Europeans. The party visited numerous towns along the route occupied by Delawares, Munsees, Mahicans, Mingos, and other Indian people dispossessed and displaced by war, epidemic disease, and land loss. Both Post and Hays recorded observations of religious rites, feasts, and drinking bouts witnessed at these towns. They also recorded a June 2nd encounter at Assinisink with a Delaware priest, whose hostility to the English and pictograph book almost surely identifies him as the prominent prophet Wangomend (Dowd 1992:32-38, Hunter 1954:76-77). Both men also documented meetings with several prisoners, sightings of others, reports of captives held elsewhere, false but nevertheless disquieting rumors of new French successes, and even more distressing real news of new murders of inoffensive Indians by vengeful frontiersmen.

Duly noting Mingo (often identified in the chronicles as *Mohaks* or *Mohaaks*) warnings not to travel beyond the headwaters of the Canisteo above the town of Secaughcung, Post and Hays further documented disturbing threats intimating that they would be roasted if the warnings were ignored. Pressing on as far as they dared, the party reached Secaughcung on June 7. Like most Susquehanna Valley Indian towns of the period, Secaughcung actually consisted of several communities. Delawares and other displaced Algonquian-speaking people lived in the lower town known as Paciksakunck or Pasekachkung (shortened by the English to Secaughcung). Mingos and other expatriate Iroquoians lived one mile upriver in the upper town named

Kaniushty or Canisteo. Europeans knew the community as a single locale, calling it either Secaughcung or Canisteo.

Situated just one day's journey south of the Seneca heartland, Secaughcung stood at a key link in the web of rivers and trails vitally important to both Indian people intent upon holding onto their lands and colonists determined to acquire them.

The party remained at Secaughcung for nearly two tense weeks before Post finally agreed to let Teedyuscung proceed on to the council alone. Turning back, Post and Hays continued to record observations of the people and places they passed until finally arriving safely at Hays's father's tavern on June 30. Post and Hays presented papers documenting their journey to provincial authorities at Bethlehem the next day. Traveling on alone, Post reached Philadelphia a couple of days later.

AFTERMATH

Events moved quickly in the region in the months following Post's return to Philadelphia. Accompanied by Tatamy, Anondounoakom, (the son of the Munsee chief at Secaughcung), Isaac Still, several other Delawares, and his own son Amos, Teedyuscung pressed on to attend the conference held in the Salt Lick Town along the headwaters of the Beaver River in present-day Niles, Ohio. In the meantime, Post acted as an interpreter in a meeting at Philadelphia from July 11 to16 with Wyalusing, Assinisink, and Secaughcung leaders honoring their promises to make peace and adjudicate differences with provincial authorities. One month later, a delegation of Upper Susquehanna Nanticoke and Conoy people living at Chenango in present-day Binghamton, New York met with Hamilton and his council in Philadelphia.

Teedyuscung and his companions came to Philadelphia on September 13. Making a formal presentation to Hamilton and his council two days later, the Delaware diplomat grandly announced that leaders of the Ottawa, Kickapoo, Kaskaskia, Miami, Wyandot, Ojibwa, Shawnee, Munsee, Western Delaware, and Mingo nations meeting with him at Salt Lick Town had agreed to make peace with the British (McConnell 1996:288). In reality, the Salt Lick Town meeting was inconsequential; the Western Nations were already meeting with Johnson's representative George Croghan at Fort Pitt. Traveling on to the Fort Pitt meeting, Teedyuscung sat silently while Tamaqua and the other Western Indian leaders concluded a formal treaty agreement ending hostilities with the Crown on August 20 (A.F.C. Wallace 1990:220-21).

As historian James Merrell affirmed in his recent survey of Pennsylvania frontier negotiation (Merrell 1999:192-93, 250), the journey accomplished little politically. Although the Indians gave up most of their captives, British intransigence and frontier vigilante violence led to a renewed outbreak of fighting in 1763. Known as Pontiac's war, the conflict lasted until 1765. Chemung Valley warriors led by the Squash Cutter and Teedyuscung's son Captain Bull played a prominent part in the struggle. The fighting did what diplomacy failed to do, irrevocably transforming the region's political landscape.

Terrorized by roving bands of frontier thugs indiscriminately murdering peaceable Indians along the frontier, Papoonan and his followers abandoned Wyalusing in the spring of 1764 (Vaughan 1984). A column of nearly 120 Tuscarora and Oneida troops led by Andrew Montour dispatched by Sir William Johnson burned all of the Chemung Valley Indian towns a few months later. Montour's report to Johnson stated that his column captured twenty-nine warriors, including Captain Bull, killed or carried off horses and cattle, and burned over 130 houses in the three towns of Secaughcung, Assinisink, and Kanawohalla. All had been abandoned as his column marched up the Forbidden Path from Tioga (Sullivan et al. 1921-65[4]:392-94).

The Indian world of the Chemung Valley, so briefly described by Post and Hays, vanished in the smoke of the fires that destroyed these towns. Farther east, contending Pennsylvanians and New Englanders took over Indian lands along the Susquehanna. Iroquois leaders signed away Delaware, Munsee, and Shawnee lands south of present-day Towanda, Pennsylvania in return for a line limiting colonial expansion west of the Allegheny Mountains at a treaty meeting with Johnson at Fort Stanwix (present-day Rome, New York) during the fall of 1768. Quickly violated by settlers, the Fort Stanwix Treaty line became one of the bones of contention that finally led to war between Great Britain and her American colonies in 1775.

Only a few of the men involved in the abortive diplomatic effort along the Forbidden Path in 1760 lived to see the outbreak of the Revolutionary War. Teedyuscung was killed in his cabin, a victim of arsonists who burned all of his people's cabins at Wyoming on 19 April, 1763. Two weeks later, New Englanders claiming no knowledge of the incident occupied Teedyuscung's town. One year later, Teedyuscung's son Captain Bull burned these and all other New England settlements he could find in the Wyoming Valley.

Tatamy died peacefully in his home at the Forks of the Delaware in 1764. Baptized by David Zeisberger one year earlier, Papoonan ended his days at the Moravian mission of Schoenbrunn in New Philadelphia, Ohio in May, 1775. Neither he nor Sir William Johnson, who passed away in his bed in his manor at Johnson Hall in present-day Johnstown on 11 July, 1774, were alive when the outbreak of the American Revolution marked the final end of the frontier world they had struggled so hard to protect and preserve.

Surrendering his governorship in 1763, James Hamilton continued to serve Pennsylvania alternately as president of the council and acting-governor until the Revolution. Although he was a devoted Loyalist, Hamilton managed to live quietly in Philadelphia throughout the war. He died on 14 August, 1783. Sir Jeffery Amherst returned to England during the winter of 1764 while the war he had done so much to instigate raged on. He declined an offer to command British forces in North America in 1775. Accepting command of all forces in England in 1778, he retired in 1783, was awarded the rank of field-marshal in 1796, and died on 3 August, 1797.

John Hays rose to the rank of captain in the Pennsylvania militia during the Revolution. Ultimately fathering 15 children, he died while on a trip viewing lands offered by Moravians in 1796. Christian Frederick Post went on to live a restlessly strenuous life. Discouraged by his unsuccessful attempt to es-tablish a Moravian mission in Ohio in 1761, he left the brethren and traveled west one year later. In 1764 he journeyed to Nicaragua, where he worked to convert Miskito Indians to Christianity. Returning to Pennsylvania three years later, he obtained Anglican support for his Mosquito Coast mission. Finally settling in the new state of Pennsylvania in 1784, he died at his home in Germantown one year later.

THE FORBIDDEN PATH CHRONICLES

William A. Hunter (1908-85) brought many forgotten and neglected manuscripts into print during a long and productive career. Born in Kinsman, Ohio, he graduated from Allegheny College and the University of California. Hunter joined the staff of the Pennsylvania Museum and Historical Commission in 1946 and served as the chief of the Commission's

INTRODUCTION

Division of History from 1961 to 1976. The prolific writer of more than one hundred scholarly publications and reports, Hunter is perhaps best remembered as the author of what is still the definitive study of Pennsylvania's French and Indian War-era forts (Hunter 1960). His updated revised edition of Paul A. W. Wallace's classic survey, *Indians in Pennsylvania* (Hunter 1981) remains a much consulted source on the subject.

Among Hunter's more intriguing and lesser known publications is an intensively edited article presenting transcriptions of John Hays's journal and diary of the trip to Secaughcung (Hunter 1954). A transcript of the carefully edited copy of Hays's journal was originally published in 1852 in the first series of the Pennsylvania Archives. (Hazard 1852b[3]:735-41). The original manuscript disappeared from its folder sometime between 1852 and 1949, when records Group 21 containing the Records of the Proprietary Government was microfilmed. Hays's far less polished diary was brought to Hunter's attention by Mrs. John C. Hays, a descendant of the militia officer, and Pennsylvania state archivist S. K. Stevens. Comparing both documents, Hunter wrote that "hurriedly written under difficult conditions, hardly legible, this diary contains many details omitted from the more composed journal" (Hunter 1954:64). Long out of print and available only in the largest or most specialized libraries, the Hays accounts have provided the only firsthand descriptions of life in the Chemung Valley Indian towns.

Twenty years later, Hunter prepared a meticulously edited copy of Christian Frederick Post's journal of the journey on file in the Historical Society of Pennsylvania in Philadelphia. The original copy of the journal "ordered to be lodged with the council papers" on 16 July, 1760 (see p. 132 below below).Three days later, WilliamLogan noted that Post had lent the journal to him. A copy also reportedly was being prepared on July 24, 1760 for British general Robert Monckton for the meeting with the Indians at Fort Pitt. Post himself wrote on August 6 that the copy for the proprietor was not yet finished.

Neither the original nor any copy of the Journal was in the possession of the state's Division of Public Records when the first series of the *Pennsylvania Archives* was published in 1852. The copy appearing in the monograph is presently curated in an individual file (Record Number AM-12605) in the collections of the Historical Society of Pennsylvania (Post 1760). The Society also holds a secondary copy of the Journal transcribed from a different original in 1859. This copy is located in the Bringhurst, Claypole, Evans, Foulke, and Parker Papers (Part II; pp. 477-95) originally held by the Genealogical Society of Pennsylvania. This copy does not differ substantively from the manuscript published here.

ASSOCIATED DOCUMENTS:

BEFORE THE JOURNEY

CHRISTIAN FREDERICK POST
TO LIEUTENANT GOVERNOR JAMES HAMILTON[1]

To his Honour the Governour:

I beg leave to lay before your Honour this short account concerning my late conversation with Teedyuscung, which I found at Fort Allen,[2] sober and well, and in obedience to your Honour's Command I have delivered the Message to him as follows, vizt:

Brother Teedyuscung, listen to what I have to say. I have it in Command from his Honour, the Governor, and from all the rest of the Gentlemen in Philadelphia, to bring you a Hearty Salutation; and a true Information also of what has happened lately near Carlisle,[3] for as much as we have a sincere desire that a good understanding may be kept up between us and the several Indian Nations, therefore the Governor sent me to you, to tell you every thing which is come to his Ears of this Affair, that it may reach yours also. So I read the proclamation.

I gave a string.

Brother Teedyuscung, we let you know by this String that we are sorry for what happened, and we assure you that the Governor and Assembly are determined to make a most diligent search into this murder, and will do all in their power to find it out, and when discovered, the authors shall be prosecuted, and if found guilty suffer death, as if they had killed an Englishman, and by this String you are desired also to give Information of the particulars thereof to the Indians about your Town, desiring them not to be disturbed or uneasy about what has happened, and assure them of our sincere and Brotherly Love towards them.

The answer of Teedyuscung to his Honour, the Governor.

March 6, 1760.

Brother: I thank you for the Message you have been pleased to send

---

[1] Published in Hazard (1852b[3]:707-09).

[2] A post built by Benjamin Franklin in 1756 near the site of the Moravian Indian mission town of Gnadenhütten destroyed in 1755 by Indians at war with the English. In present-day Weissport, Pennsylvania, near the Lehigh Gap.

[3] I.e., the murder of Delaware Doctor John and his wife and children by a settler.

me by Mr. Frederick Post. I have heard and understood him well, and your Pain and Care which you have shown in this Affair pleases me very much and gives me satisfaction.

Brother: I let you know I cannot say much about it now. 'Tis true there are many rogues on both sides: it grieves and troubles me and who knows who has done it, if the white people or the Indians, neither you nor I can tell the authors. It is as much concern to me as it is to you to see that the Peace and Chain[4] shall not be broken.

Brother: be strong, see to find out the Authors of the Murder.

Brother: I am not willing to stay much longer here, and I do not like to go from here home, until I have seen you, and laid my Hand in yours, then we will confer more about this Affair, & we will see to bury it under Ground,[5] that it shall not be seen, for fear it remains too long some rogues will find occasion to do some mischief. This is the reason I hasten, and I think to see you in three weeks hence. I salute the Governor and all the Gentlemen.

He gave this String.

Further he told me that one of his Emissary's was come home, and had brought news that the Minisink Indians were gathered at Schemanga,[6] and intend to come down to renew and brighten the Chain of Friendship by bringing their Prisoners down themselves about 6 Weeks hence. I wish it may be so. I had many agreeable conversations with him, and found him well disposed.

FREDERICK POST

Bethlehem, 11th March, 1760.

Please your Honour, for as much as this present undertaking of my going to the great council of the different Nations goes very neare to my Heart, desiring God our Heavenly Father to grant his aid and grace, that it may turn out according to his holy will, and the glory of our gracious Sovereign, and to the Honour of the Governor, Council and Assembly, and all men in power under him, and to the advantage and safety not only of the Inhabitants of this Province, but of all his Majesties Loiale Subjects on this

---

[4] A reference to the symbolic covenant chain alliance joining the English with their Indian allies.

[5] An Indian metaphor symbolizing resolution of a problem.

[6] Munsee Indians originally from the lower Hudson and upper Delaware Valleys then living along the upper Susquehanna River Valley. Schemanga refers to the Chemung River region in present-day south-central New York.

Continent, that Peace may be made with these numerous and dangerous Indian Nations, which by all probability is the wisest step which men in power at this juncture can take and wish for. Therefore it is fallen in my minde that it would be good and necessary, if your Honour would be pleased, to let General Amherst know of my going to their Council, For I think it would be of great consequence, both to the Province and to the Indians; if I had a word to bring theym from the Chief Commander of all his Majesties Forces here, for I am sure they will aske me very closely to tell them the real truth of the intention of our great warior and chief in regard to theym who is sent from the king to this Country to act in his Name. For the Indians will much listen to what hope of advantage a Messenger will geave them from the Chief Roolers. I know one of theire Principall Point in theire Council will be, how to secure the limits between them and they white people, so that they may live by theymselfs a due distance from us, to secure theire hunting ground, for they are more affraid of loosing theire hunting grounds than theire lives and they are very much preposest and suspicous that is our scheme to incroge upon them, and spoile theire hunting, and bring them in messery and slavery, and they like the Jews think we are free born and no slaves, and will therefore rather die than submit to worck. I for my part, doubt not at all but that they Indians will grant a tract of land for a trading plaes, in a proper manner bought of them and while they white people don't hount on land which is not bought of them, and in so doing one can avoide all quarrels with theym else it wou'd not be safe for anny one to live upon theire land otherwise, for my part I can never see trough how a peace can be settled with the Indians. To root theym out or subdue theym I think it is impossible for this thime, for theire is not one who rightly knows there Country and theare lurking holes an there severall Nations and strength.

Please your Honour not to take it amiss of me that I write my opinion and thoughts about this Affair, I do it out of a sincere and honest Heart, according to my knolege for the best and wellfare of the public I submit to your Honour's superior judgment, an am, with due respect,

Your Honour's

Most humble and

Obedeant Servt.,

CHRISTIAN FREDERICK POST.

Bethm, March the 11th, 1760.

19

CHRONICLES OF A DIPLOMATIC MISSION

PENNSYLVANIA PROVINCIAL COUNCIL MINUTES[7]

At a Council held at Philadelphia, Saturday the 29th March, 1760.

Present:

The Honourable · JAMES HAMILTON, Esquire, Lieutenant Governor.

William Logan,   Richard Peters,
Lynford Lardner,   Benjamin Chew, Esquires

Indians Present:

Teedyuscung, the Delaware Chief,
Moses Tettamy.
Frederick Post,
Moses Tettamy, Interpreters.

The Governor informed the Council that Teedyuscung was in Town, and by Fred'k Post, his interpreter, had acquainted him he had a Great many things to say to the Governor of a publick nature, & desired the assembly might be present when he spoke; whereupon the Governor having been told before hand the substance of what he had to say, sent his secretary with a verbal message to the House informing them of this, and desiring their attendance, with the speaker, in the Council chamber, who accordingly came, &, on their taking their seats, Teedyuscung spoke as follows:
"Brother:

"I received a Message from you by Frederick Post, who took me by the Hand and brought me here, and I am now standing ready before the Governor to confer within on the subject of his Message."
"Brother:

"I always desire that when I speak I may be well understood, and if in the delivery of what I speak I should, thro' my want of proper expression, commit any mistake, I desire it may be taken notice of, and forthwith set right, that no harm may accrue thereby to our children and Grand children."

A String.
"Brother:

"I request of you and all present to give serious attention to what I am going to say.

"You know that our hands are joined fast together, and we are entered into close Alliance and Friendship with each other, and that we have agreed if any accident should happen which might tend to a breach of our

---

[7] Published in Hazard, ed. 1852a[8]:463-67.

Union, we should use our speediest and best endeavors to prevent it.
"Brother:

"Since we last one another last, something has happened whereby our union is struck and wounded. There lye some dead bodies between us, uncovered on the ground, which fill our hearts with Grief and our Eyes with Tears, so that we can neither see nor speak to one another until they be put out of our sight.
"Brother:

"I am poor and you are able, but poor as I am I will nevertheless put forth my strength to cover these dead Bodies, that no mischief may arise from their lying too long uncovered. In this I call upon you to help me, as you are more able than I am.[8] Let us, I say, both join heartily and speedily to cover these dead Bodies, that neither the Neighbouring Indians nor those who live at a distance may take offence at them, but be satisfied that we have done right, and everything that such an occasion requires."

A String.

Then, after some pause, taking a string of Wampum, he proceeded saying:
"Brother:

"I received this string from Atsuntsing,[9] with a message from the Indians residing there, acquainting me that they and all the other Indians on the river Susquehannah are determined to observe what their Brethren, the English, requested of them, and desired I would assure you of their Friendship towards you, and that they would be watchful and take a special care that no more mischief be done, nor more Horses carried off."

A String.

Then taking another String of Wampum, he spoke further:
"Brother:

"I received this string from the Mohiccon and Oping Indians,[10] with a message to desire I would let their Brethren, the English, know that they had heard of the peace which you and I had made together, and were heartily glad to hear of it, and would do their best to promote the good work & join with me in everything that I should agree upon with our Brethren, the English."

---

[8] Teedyuscung is using key Indian diplomatic metaphors, representing uncondoled murders as uncovered bodies and reminding his allies that he needed presents to condole the grieving relatives of the murder victims.

[9] Assinisink, "Rocky Place," at present-day Corning, New York. See p. 8.

[10] Mahican and Wappinger people originally from the Hudson River Valley then living in Upper Susquehanna country.

A String.

"Brother:

"When I speak to my Brethren, I speak from my heart, & with sincerity, and whilst I do, the Great God who made us will bless me: I expect you will act the same part by me, & then the great God will bless you likewise. Whoever of us should act a part contrary to this, will certainly be discovered, and looked upon as the Author of the Breach, and answerable for all the evils that it will occasion. Let us, therefore, on both sides take care to be very sincere to one another, that the Great God may bless both of us, and what we do may be well established, and prove very lasting."

A String.

Then, taking out a Belt of nine rows of Wampum, which was about Two feet long, on which a Road was described as passing thro' twelve Towns, he spoke further:

"Brother:

"I received this Belt from all the Warriors and young Men who live on the Sasquehannah River, with a message, pressing me to be Strong, and telling me they would reach out their hands and lift me on my legs, and desired I would be with them in Six weeks, and they would collect themselves together from all their Towns, and meet at atsunsing, and there hold a Council before my going to the great Council over the River Ohio. These Young warriors further desired me to let all the Indians know wherever I come, that they were determined to sit still and strictly observe the peace and Friendship entered into with the English, and would do no more mischief, and they desired of all the Indians in the several places through which I should pass, that they would act the same part. Now, Brother, I desire that since these Warriors have promised to help me on, you would likewise do the same, and be strong, and make me able to perform this great journey.

"Brother:

"I desire Frederick Post may not go single, but that I may take another white man with me, as well as he, and then, if any thing happens to him, the other, who will be acquainted with every part of our Business, may assist me to carry it on. If you will deliver these to me I will put them in my Bosom; I will cover them from all harm, and see them safe returned. I have, also, desired moses Tattamy may be one of these Indians who are to accompany me.

"Brother:

"There are two or three old men here who are to accompany me; as they are not able to travel on foot such a great way, I expect you will provide them and me with Horses and other necessaries; and as I shall have a great [many] messages to send, and a great many speeches to make, I expect you will provide me with a sufficient quantity of Wampum."

Some black Strouds, Handkerchiefs, and Stockings, having been provided, the Governor ordered them to be spread upon the floor, and then spoke as follows:
"Brother Teedyuscung:
"I mean to answer only that part of your speech which relates to the dead Bodies; the rest will be answered at another time.
"Brother:
"It pleases me that you have taken the trouble to come down so quickly, and join your endeavors with mine in Clearing the ground from the Blood, and burying the Bones in utter Oblivion.

"As soon as we were made acquainted with what had happened, we took all the pains in our power to find out the authors; The Assembly joined with me in offering a very large Reward; the proclamation sent you was instantly published & dispersed in every part of the province, & Sheriffs & magistrates were every where industrious to find it out. Hitherto we have not been able to make a discovery; but you may be assured that we shall continue to use our utmost endeavors, & if the authors are detected and found Guilty, they shall suffer death in the Same manner as if they killed one of our own people.
"Brother:
"According to your advice I am now going on the part of this Government, and all his majestie's Subjects, to join with you in removing these and all other dead Bodies that lye on the Earth between us uncovered, out of our sight. I put my hand to yours and bury them all deep in the Ground, that it should not be in any one's power to dig them up again and expose them to view. In confirmation whereof, I give you this String.
"Brother:
"I wipe the Tears from your Eyes and remove all Grief from your heart, and enable you to speak again. Let us now think no more of what has passed. Let it be buried in Oblivion forever."
    A String.
"Brother:
"I desire you will repeat what I have now said to the Indians present, Some of whom, I understand, you intend to take with you, that they may be well informed of all these particulars, and I desire that both you and they will be careful to make them known in all places wherever you come, especially at

the great Council where you are going to attend at their pressing invitation."

Teedyuscung turned himself to the Indians, & with a very particular warmth, repeated all that had passed, & desired them to take notice of it & be witnesses at the ensuing council of the care taken by the Governor & him to bury the dead Bodies, and of what his Honour had mentioned with respect to the pains taken & rewards offered for the discovery of the murderers.

At a Council held at Philadelphia,
Thursday, the third of April, 1760.

Present:

The Honourable JAMES HAMILTON, Esquire, Lieutenant Governor.
William Logan,
Richard Peters, Esquires
Joseph Fox,
Jno. Hughes, Provincial Commissioners
Teedyuscung & the Indians.
Moses Tattamy,
Frederick Post, Interpreters.

The Governor having sent to the Assembly the draught of his answer to make to Teedyuscung, and a Present of Goods having been provided by the Provincial Commissioners, he is to give them an answer to the remainder of his speeches delivered on Saturday, and then spoke as follows:
"Brother:

"I am glad to hear of the good dispositions of the Indians at Atsunsing and in all other Towns on the Sasquehannah, & especially with the determination of the young Warriors to observe the peace.
"Brother:

"You are extreamly well acquainted with the particulars of all the Transactions that have passed as well as of all the Treaties that have been held between us, and as you are our agent and Councellor, by this Belt I enable you to speak for us on all Occasions, make known our good disposition and love towards all the Indians wherever you go; Hide nothing from them; spread the knowledge of what We have been doing far & wide, and dispose them, as you shall have an opportunity of conversing with them, to enter into the peace, and join heartily with us to settle every thing on the most lasting foundation."

A String.

"Brother:

"I am very Sensible that the Business you are engaged in is of the greatest importance, and in transacting it you will be obliged to make many Speeches, and to send many Messages to different Indian Towns, which can't be done without a great Quantity of Wampum. I have, therefore, put into your Council Bag, as much Wampum as we hope will enable you to discharge every part of your duty."

Here gave the Wampum.

"Brother:

"Your requesting another person to accompany you, besides Mr. Post, convinces me that you have the business you are engaged in, much at heart. I heartily concur with you in this measure, and shall appoint another, who shall be agreeable to you both; and as the journey will be long, I have, as you requested, provided you with Horses, and all necessaries for the Journey, of which the Provincial commissioners have my Orders to deliver you."

"Brother:

"I put Mr. Post, and the other Assistant, into your care & protection; Take them with you wherever you go, to bring them safe back again, and I hope you will consult with Mr. Post on all occasions, and make him fully acquainted with every thing that shall pass."

A String.

"Brother:

"There is one point I think incumbent on me to mention particularly to you, and to insist in behalf of all his majestie's Subjects within this province, that you spare no pains to see it speedily and effectually complyed with.

"You cannot but remember it was solemnly stipulated by you in all our treaties, that our Flesh and Blood who have been carried into Captivity, should be very carefully collected and delivered to us. We are sensible of the kind part you have taken in this affair, and thank you for it; But we are obliged, with Grief, to take notice that the prisoners brought to us are very few, in comparison with the Great numbers who remain still in captivity. By this Belt, therefore, we earnestly desire of you to make this known to all Indians wherever you shall go, and to use your endeavors that all the English prisoners be collected and delivered to us, otherwise We cannot think the professions made to us of peace and Friendship can be sincere."

A Belt.

Teedyuscung returned the Governor thanks for his kind speeches, acknowledged his Satisfaction at the great trust that was reposed in him, and promised that he would do everything that should be in his power, and prayed almighty God to assist him; he added that if he returned safe home he would continue to do everything he could for the service of his Brethren.

The Governor thanked Teedyuscung, and at taking his leave he said to the Governor:

"Brother:

"You have really covered the dead. I will make it known wherever I go. I will do with all the nations I shall see as you have done with me, and send you their Approbation and hearty concurrence with you and me in this Affair."

The Secretary having prepared the draught of a set of Instructions to Mr. Frederick Post, the same were read and settled, and are as follows:

"Instructions to Mr. Frederick Post, assigned at Teedyuscung's request to accompany and assist him in his Journey to a Great council of Indians proposed to be held at some principal Indian Town over the Ohio.

"You are tõ take all the care in your power, that Teedyuscung sets out time enough to be present at the opening of the Council, and that he takes with him the Wampum given him to use on this Occasion, and if more be wanting and can be purchased, you have liberty to supply him out of the money you will receive from the Provincial Commissioners, or if that cannot be spared, you may assure such as will part with Wampum, it shall be replaced or paid for by me.

"Copies of all the Treaties and Conferences with Teedyuscung, and other Indians, down to this time, are made out, and will be delivered you together with these Instructions, that you may be able to remind Teedyuscung of every material thing that has been transacted, and I expect you will pay a particular attention to this important part of your service.

"I approve of the detail of Affairs made by you in your last Journey over the Ohio, and would have the same again distinctly repeated at this great

Council, together with what has been done since, for the benefit of such distant Indians as may never have the like opportunities of hearing such a true relation of these matters.

"You are to observe and perform all the ceremonies expected by and in use among the Indians, from persons when they spake on publick matters, and enforce all your speeches with proper Belts or Strings of Wampum.

"You are to assure the Indians of our sincere disposition towards peace, and that we shall do our utmost Endeavors not only to renew and strengthen our friendship and Alliances, but to settle everything to their Satisfaction that is likely to occasion differences, and shall observe and promote such a friendly, affectionate and brotherly Confidence as will preserve a mutual and lasting Esteem and Regard for each other.

"You are to acquaint the Indians in the name of the General and Commander-in-Chief of all his majestie's forces in North America, that, according to the request of the Indians in their message by Pisquitomeng,[11] which was received during the last treaty at Easton, His Majesty King George has been truly informed of all The transactions between the Indians & his majesty's subjects, and our Gracious King, as a tender Father over all his children, was much pleased to hear of your good disposition, & has given orders to his Generals & Governors, that agreeable to your request, there should be a General Peace established between the Indians and his subjects in every colony on a Good and firm foundation, and they Will all endeavor with zeal to promote this good work.

"You are further, in the General's name, to relate what passed in the Conference between the Generals, the Governors of this and the neighbouring provinces and the Indians' Deputies from Caghnawago,[12] in April, 1759, agreeable the minutes of which you have a Copy, and assure the Indians that His excelency will faithfully perform what he then promised, and expects the same from them; you are, if you arrive safe at the Council, to express high satisfaction in finding the road from this province to their Towns perfectly safe and easy to be travelled in, and you are to take care in the strongest manner to assure the Indians that the road from their Country to this City is entirely open and safe for them to travel in, as they have been repeatedly invited by this Government in conjunction with Teedyuscung, to come to this City, where the Old Council Fire was first kindled, and Till of

---

[11] Pisquitomen was an influential Delaware diplomat. McConnell (1996) presents an account of his political career.

[12] Caughnawaga, near present-day Montreal, Quebec.

late was constantly burning, you will learn what their intentions are, and, if necessary, you will advise Teedyuscung to invite them once more in our joint names to come to this Council Fire, and if they agree to it, then you will proceed to fix the number of Deputies and the time of their coming, that we may lay in sufficient Provisions and be prepared to receive them.

"You are sensible, as Indians cannot be kept from drink, it would be both troublesome and dangerous to their health to have great numbers come down to the Treaty, it is to be wished therefore, and you are to endeavor to bring it about, that a certain respectable number of their principal Men as well as Warriors as Members of their Councils may be deputed to appear and act for the injured in their Lands or any ways concerned in the Complaints made at Easton, may come down with the Deputies, and furnished with full powers for that purpose.

"This is a tender point, and will require Skill & Prudence; but for the above, and many other reasons that will occur to you, it should be pressed as far as you can venture to do it.

"The Indian chiefs have often heretofore, and Teedyuscung at his last Conference, earnestly desired that a Stop might be put to the sending such excessive Quantitys of Rum Into the Indian Country, and that at Treaties especially particular care might be taken to prevent Indians getting it.

"You will occasionally acquaint the Indians, if this matter be mentioned, that we have many Good Laws for the regulation of this matter, which will ever prove insufficient whilst the Indians themselves give such encouragement to this Vice, and by means of their own people carry on such underhand practices for the purchase of Rum, as render it impossible for us to detect the Offenders; the Chiefs must, if they really mean to preserve their health and do publick business in a right manner, lay proper restraints on their own people, and stave every cask that is brought into their Country; this is in their power, and till this be done on their part, all our care will prove ineffectual.

"You are to recollect every thing that has been said from time to time with respect to the Surrender of all our Prisoners, and to take care to find out what number of our fellow subjects have been carried into captivity, their Names, Ages, whence taken, where they are now to be found, and how they are treated by the Indians; & learn every circumstance relating to them, and the real disposition of the Indians as to the delivery of them.

"As the Captives become private properties, and are often adopted into Families in the room of deceased Relations, I am sensible that great art will be used in keeping back many of our Captives, & perhaps some of them would not be willing to come, and therefore earnestly recommend it to you to find out with Teedyuscung the properest way of removing all these difficulties, so that this which we have so much at heart may be effectually performed.

"Lastly: You will give the Indians every where the strongest assurances that no person shall be permitted to make Settlements on their land, or any where to the Westward of the Allegheny Mountains; acquaint them that a Law has already passed in this Government forbidding our inhabitants from hunting or killing Game in any of their hunting Grounds, under severe penalties; and that the General will be told of this, and desired to give it in charge to all the Officers and Soldiers to see this Law put in execution.

"This they will consider as a very strong testimony of our faithful observance of our promises to the Indians on this head.

"I heartily recommend you to the care of devine providence, praying that he may afford you Strength and health to perform this great and important Trust."

GENERAL SIR JEFFERY AMHERST
TO LIEUTENANT GOVERNOR JAMES HAMILTON[13]

New York, 30th March, 1760.

I come now, Sir, to your Letter in relation to Indian Affairs, and cannot but commend your attention in keeping up a Friendship and Trade with all such Indians as chuse to partake of the Blessings of the happy Government we live under; And your proposal of sending Mr. Post & Mr. Still to assist at the large Convention reported to you by Teedyuscung, to be held in the Spring, at some of the Indian Towns over the Ohio, is, I think perfectly right, as it may be productive of Cemmenting the Alliance that ought to subsist between these Nations and Us; and as I have nothing more at heart, than the good and welfare of the whole Community, and that Mr. Post thinks it necessary he should carry them a talk from His Majesty's Commander in chief, to Assure them that it is not our Design to make any encroachments among them, but on the contrary protect and Defend their Lives and Properties; I will here renew, what I promised at a Conference held in April last, at Philadelphia, between Govrs Denny, Bernard, De Lancey,

---

[13] Extract from a letter published in Hazard (1852b[3]:716-17). A copy also exists in the papers of Sir William Johnson and is published in Sullivan et al. (1921-65[3]:204-06).

Brigr Genl Stanwix & myself, the Deputies of Canawaga & Thomas King,[14] of which I enclose you a Copy; And I shall further add, what I have from time to time wrote to Sr Wm. Johnson, to deliver to the Indians, in his Department on my behalf, vizt., That His Majesty had not sent me to deprive any of them of their Lands & Property; on the contrary, that so long as they adhered to his interest, and by their behaviour gave proofs of the sincerity of their Attachment to his Royal Person & Cause, I should defend and maintain them in their Just Rights, and give them all the Aid & Assistance they might stand in need of, to repress the Dangers they might be liable to from the Enemy, thro' their Attachment to us. This I firmly mean to adhere to, so long as their Conduct shall deserve it; but on the other hand, if they do not behave as good and faithful allies ought to do, and renounce all Acts of Hostility against His Majesty's Subjects, I shall retaliate upon them, and have the might to do so, tenfold every breach of treaty they shall be guilty of, and every Outrage they shall Committ; and if any of His Majesty's Subjects under my Command, should kill or injure any of our Indian brethren, they shall, upon due proof thereof, receive equal punishment. I mean not neither to take any of their lands, Except in such cases Where the necessity of His Majesty's Service Obliges me to take Post, Where I must & will build Forts; but then the Lands adjoining will still continue their own, and be not only equally good for their hunting, but be so much the more secure against any interruption the Enemy might offer to give them, for I know no medium between us & the French, if We have not Forts they will. Those that will join His Majesty's arm, and that will be Aiding & Assisting in Subduing the Common Enemy, shall be well rewarded; And those that may not Chuse to Act in Conjunction with the Forces, shall be equally protected, Provided they do not Join in any Acts of Hostility with the Enemy, or Carry them Intelligence, which might prove prejudicial to the Publick good. Upon these terms they shall find me their fast friend, but on a breach of them I shall punishing them as they Deserve, and I Chuse they should know what they have to trust to, since I intend to be as good as my word.

I am, with great regard, Sir,

Your most obedient,

Humble Servant

JEFF.AMHERST

Honr. Governor Hamilton

---

[14] A reference to the treaty attended by then Pennsylvania Lieutenant Governor William Denny, New Jersey Governor Francis Bernard, New York Governor James De Lancey, Brigadier General John Stanwix, representatives of the Caughnawaga mission Indian community near Montreal, and the Oneida speaker and diplomat Thomas King.

LIST OF NECESSARIES TO BE PROVIDED FOR TEEDYUSCUNG[1]

31st March, 1760.

A List of necessaries to be provided for Teedyuscung and his Company:

Teedyuscung is to be fitted out with a good suit of Cloathes, Hat, &c., that he may make an Appearance answerable to the Occasion.

Mr. Frederick Post recommends it to the Governor to send Presents to consist of some silver Ornaments to King Beaver, Chingas, Custalogo, Netonetamet, Delaware George, and a few other Chiefs, who have been and may be serviceable to us.

Queetahickon, Nutimus & Packsenosa, who will go with Teedyuscung should have each a Strowd[2] & a Shirt sent to them.

A small present is to be made to the Indians who are now in Town, such as shall be thought proper:

2 Dozen of Shirts,
2 Dozen of Handkerchiefs,
1 Dozen Blankets,
1 Dozen Strowds,
2 Dozen Pair of Stockings,
1 Dozen Breech Clout,
12 Pair of Shoes,
12 Hats,
2 Half Barrels of Powder,
    Lead in Proportion,
30 lb. Swanshot & Pigeon shot,[3]
3 Good, strong Horses,
2 Bells for Horses with
    Hopples and Halters,[4]
Horseshoes and Nails,
Vermillion,
Knives,
Ribbons,
Awls,
Needles and Thread,

Tinder Box and Steele,
Flints,
Osnabrig[5] for Baggs & Wallets,
Leather to mend shoes,
2 Kettles,
10 Tin Cupps,
1 Pound of Tea,
3 Pound of Chocolate and Sugar,
Half Pound of Pepper,
½ Bushel of Salt,
2 Axes,
Flower,[6]
Biscuit,
Cheese,
Writing Paper,
Gunns,
Soap,
Saddle-Bags for Mr. Post,
Pipes and Tobacco.

1st April, 1760.

---

[1] Published in Hazard (1852b[3]:717-18).

[2] I.e., a stroudswater wool blanket.

[3] I.e., small buck-shot.

[4] I.e., hobbles for restraining horses and halters for their necks.

[5] Coarse wool.

[6] I.e., flour.

CHRONICLES OF A DIPLOMATIC MISSION

VOTE OF THE PENNSYLVANIA PROVINCIAL ASSEMBLY [1]

April 1, 1760.

The Governor, by Mr. Secretary, sent down to the House a copy of Christian Frederick Post's Letter, containing an Account of the Delivery of the Governor's Proclamation and Messages to Teedyuscung; also a Copy of his Honour's Conference with Teedyuscung, in the State House on the Twenty-ninth ult. With a Draught of his proposed Answer thereto, and a List of Necessaries required by Frederick Post for Teedyuscung's intended journey to Atsunsing, and the Great Council of Indians soon to be held on the Ohio, which said several Papers were read, and being duly considered,

Ordered, That Mr. Fox and Mr. Leech wait on the Governor, and acquaint him, the House are obliged to his Honour for the Papers laid before them, that they entirely approve his intended Answer to Teedyuscung's Speech, and will recommend to the Provincial Commissioners to furnish the Necessaries required for his Journey.

GENERAL SIR JEFFERY AMHERST TO SIR WILLIAM JOHNSON [2]

at New York, 2 April, 1760.

The last Post brought me a Letter from Govr. Hamilton, Acquainting me that Teedyuscung had Informed him, there was to be, this Spring, a very large Convention of Indians, in some of their Towns on the Ohio, at which he was to Assist, in behalf of the Province of Pennsylvania, and desired that Mr. Frederick Post might Accompany him; that at the instance pf Teedyuscung, the Assembly of Pennsylvania had Named said Mr Post and One Mr. Still, to Attend this Chief of the Delawares; And that Mr. Post had represented, that his being the Bearer of a Talk from His Majesty's Commander in Chief, to the Several Tribes of Indians that should Come to this Meeting, might be productive of great good Consequence to His Majesty's Indian Interest in those parts: Accordingly I Sent him the Enclosed

---

[1] Published in MacKinney and Hoban (1931-35[6]:521-22).
[2] Extract from a letter published in Sullivan et al. (1921-65[3]:207).

32

Answer,[3] by which You will See my Invariable Sentiments in relation to Indians, in which I intend ever to persevere.

TEEDYUSCUNG TO SIR WILLIAM JOHNSON[4]

at Bethlehem, 8 April, 1760.

Brother, I rec'd Your Letter by my son[5] and was glad to hear that King George has been so good to take my matters to heart, and I thank you for your love and care in sending me so early word. But as I am to morrow setting off from here, being desired by the Governor and other Gentlemen of this Province to the Wiandot Nation & others, to invite and convene them to a Treaty at Easton. Therefore at present I can neither appoint time or place to confer about the complaint I made about Land affairs, But when I return shall take the first opportunity to let you know, & am Your sincere Brother, that wishes you good luck against his Majesties Enemies.

Tydescung Chief Sachem of the Delawares,
his mark

PASSPORT FOR CHRISTIAN FREDERICK POST, TEEDYUSCUNG, ETC.[6]

By the Honourable JAMES HAMILTON, Esquire, Lieutenant Governor and Commander in Chief of the Province of Pennsylvania, and Counties of Newcastle, Kent and Sussex, on Delaware.
To all to whom these Presents shall come, Greeting:

Whereas, Mr. Frederick Post and Mr. John Hayes, together with Moses Tettamy and Isaac Stille, have undertaken, at the request of Teedyuscung, to bear him Company in his Journey to several distant Indian Nations, with whom he is to hold Treaties, and in consequence thereof is charged with matters of great Importance, as well as by the General of his Majesty's Forces as by this Government, and they have requested my Letters of Passport, Protection, & Safe Conduct, not only for themselves but for all

---

[3] The March 30 letter from Amherst to Hamilton published above.

[4] Published in O'Callaghan and Fernow (1853-87[7]:436-37).

[5] Copies of this letter, informing Teedyuscung of the King's order that Johnson adjudicate outstanding Delaware land claims, are published in (Hazard 1852b[8]:507), O'Callaghan (1849-51[2]:789-90), and Sullivan et al. (1925-65[3]:194-95).

[6] Published in Hazard (1852b[3]:720-21).

other persons, both White Men and Indians, whom they may find necessary to take with them on this Occasion; Sensible of the merit and of the great Trust reposed in the said Frederick Post, John Hayes, Moses Tettamy, and Isaac Stille, I do most readily grant them these my Letters of Passport, Protection, and Safe Conduct, requiring and desiring all Officers, Civil and Military, & all other Persons whatever, to afford them all necessary Aid & Assistance in passing and repassing to and from the Indian Country; And as they may find occasion, either to come or send other Persons with Messages to the General, or to Me, or any other of his Majesty's Governors, I do most earnestly recommend it to the Officers who may have the chief Command in any Posts or Places thro' which they may pass, to receive them kindly, & to furnish them with Provisions & necessary Escorts, that they may be enabled to deliver their Dispatches with expedition. Given under my Hand and the Lesser Seal of the said Province, at Philadelphia, this twenty second day of April, 1760.

THE JOURNAL OF CHRISTIAN FREDERICK POST
APRIL 21 - JUNE 30, 1760

Journal of Mr Christn. Fred Post, in Company with Teedyuscung,
Mr John Hays, Isaac Still, & Moses Tattamy, to the great Council
of the different Indian Nations, 1760

April [2]1st Return'd to Philadelphia, being somewhat recovered from the
Dangerous Accident I met with on my Way to New York.

[April] 22nd I received my Instructions from his Honour the Governor.
Afterwards I visited Mr. Logan, & Colonel Boquet,[1] with whom I conferr'd
about preparing a Writing to his Excellency General Amherst, concerning his
message to the Indians.

[April] 23rd. I spoke with the Commissioners, by whom it was agreed on, that
Moses Tattamy should go alone to Teedyuscung to acquaint him of the
Misfortune that had befallen me, & that Isaac Still sho'd wait for the
Generals Answer. To my surprise Moses Tattamy & Isaac Still both came to
take leave of me, to go to Teedyuscung, which troubled me, as I feared it wo'd
be attended with bad Consequences, Nevertheless I deliver'd them the
Message & String of Wampum from the Governor.

[April] 29th. I was sent for to the Governor, from whom I had the Honour to
receive the agreeable Answer & Message from his Excellency General
Amherst, that had been settled & agreed upon by him, which contained such
solid & essential Articles, that a firm & lasting Peace may, by Means thereof
be reasonably establish'd, with the different Indian Nations.

May 2nd. I waited on the Provincial Commissioners & laid all my Messages
& matters I was intrusted with before them, with which they were all well
satisfy'd & pleased. Teedyuscungs Son Capt. Bull & another young Indian
from Allegeny, happen'd to be there at the Time, and directly agreed to
Accompany me as far as Allegeny.

---

[1] The Mr. Logan mentioned by Post may have been provincial councillor William Logan, or
his brother, James Logan, Jr. (see Stevens, et al. 1972-94[4]:467nn.). Colonel Boquet was Swiss
soldier of fortune Henry Bouquet. Best known for his relief of Pittsburgh after pressing
through the besieging Indian force following the Battle of Bushy Run three years later,
Bouquet's biography and collected papers may be consulted in Stevens, et al. (1972-94)

[May] 3rd. We presented them before his Honour the Governor, who gave Order that they sho'd be well fitted out for their Journey. We then took Leave, his Honour wishing that the Lord God might be with us, give us Success in our Undertaking & a safe & prosperous Return.

This Day I found myself very Weak & faint with the hurry & fateigue in preparing for my Journey, yet I set out in the Evening abt. 6 oClock. Mr. Israel Pemberton[2] was so kind as to lend me his Chaise, & Mr. L. Weiss to conduct me to Bethlehem. It was late before we reach'd Germantown, where we lodged at Machenets.

[May] 4th. Rose early, & finding myself very Weak, I wrote to Mr. Pemberton, to desire to procure me a Tent. After which I went out to seek the Indians, who were to go with me, & found them Sober & well at the King of Prusia. Having Breakfasted we proceeded on our Journey. As I had several old Accounts of Teedyuscung to Pay off in the Taverns along ye Road, Capt. Bull went before, but unfortunately took the wrong Road, so was oblidg'd to send an Express to bring him back, we reach'd that Evening to Saml. Deans.

[May] 5th. We set out very early & came that Day safe & well to Bethlehem. I immediately dispatched a Messenger to Mr. Hays & inform'd of what I had in Commission.

[May] 6th. I was inform'd there had been some Disturbance among the Indians at Fort Allen,[3] on account, they having been told by Moses Tattamy, that he had Instructions & Orders to carry the Message without delay, & that he need not wait for any body else. This I fear'd would create me many Difficulties.

[May] 7th. To Day I was busily employ'd preparing to prosecute my Journey. Mr. Pemberton sent me a Horse, two Belts of Wampum & a Tent, for which I was exceedingly glad & Thankful.

---

[2] The leading Quaker politician in Philadelphia at the time.

[3] Weissport, Pennsylvania. See ff. 2, p. 16.

JOHN HAYS' JOURNAL, MAY 5 - JUNE 30, 1760

Monday May 5th 1760. Received A Letter from Mr. Post with orders to be in Readiness, and to come down Next Day to Bethlehem to See him-

May 6th. Tuesday went to Bethlehem and saw Mr. Post, who told me he would be at my fathers[1] the Eight, consulted about fitting out, and so Returned the same night

[May] 7th. Wednesday Spent the Day in Getting Ready to go

---

[1] Hays's Tavern, in present-day Weaversville, in Northampton County, Pennsylvania

[May] l8th. I hurried to get away To Day, but could not get further than Hay's where I found my Companion ready. Several Things which Moses Tattamy had left in his Drunken Fits, I found & took with me.

[May] 9th. I found myself weak & poorly & co.d not travel to Day without great Inconveniency & Pain; In the Evening I reach'd Fort Allen.[4] Here they related to me how badly the Goods had been managed, that were sent up for the Indians, they having divided them amongst them, & already squandered away a good many of them, which I was much grieved to hear. I thought to have procured here what I yet wanted for my Journey, but was disappointed; I was oblig'd to leave off writing, my Head growing so giddy, & lie down to rest.

[May] 10th. In the Fort we were treated with the best the Place afforded, & taking our Leave of them, as the last White Inhabitants, we committed our selves to the Care & protection of our heavenly Father to guide & provide for us on our Way. We cross'd the Lehi 3 times to Day, the Water being so rapid made me frequently so giddy that I was oblig'd to cling fast to my Horse & look up to God for his help & assistance, who brot. me safely thro'. We came over the two Nishywashowall, two high Mountains, and afterwards cross'd the Meskonekong which runs between two Meadows.[5] When we ascended the great Mountain on the other side, all my Limbs trembled as if I had a fit of the Ague,[6] & in descending the same it made both Man & Beast tremble. At the foot of the Hill we cross'd a Creek, called Quakake,[7] with Steep Banks. My horse being formerly a Gentleman's & not used to such hardships & to climb such craggy Hills & steep Mountains, laid himself twice flat on the ground with me, yet I came happily off without much hurt, save bruising my Leggs against the Stones. We travell'd till late in the Evening & came to the Creek Memendag,[8] where we encamp'd that Night. I boil'd Coffee for our Refreshment.

---

[4] See ff. 2, p. 17.

[5] Nishywashowall and the Meskonekong may refer to the Mahoning and Nesquehoning Creeks. The name Meskonekong "swiftly flowing river," is also affixed to the Musconetcong River in western New Jersey. The party's route here almost certainly followed what Paul A. W. Wallace (1965:113-14) later identified as the Nescopeck Path.

[6] The term ague, and especially trembling or tertian ague, was often used to identify the symptoms of malaria during this period.

[7] Today the name of a creek, township, and hill in Carbon County. The Nescopeck Path crosses Quakake Creek at present-day Hudsonville (P.A.W. Wallace 1965:113-14). The name probably means "pine tree place" (Donehoo 1928:165).

[8] The identity of this creek is unknown.

[May 8th] & Thursday Got my Horse Shod and waited Mr. Posts comeing, who came in the Evening.

Freday [May] 9th. Set out Early and arrived at ffort Allen.[2]

Saturday [May] 10th. Heasie wether; Set off from fort Allen at Eight o Clock, and traveled till it was Late through a vast Desert; Lodged in the Woods.

---

[2] See ff. 2, p. 17.

[May] 11th. It is hard to stay in a Place where there is little Food for the Horses, especially the First Night. This Circumstance occasion'd us to spend half the Day in hunting up the Horses. I had a very friendly Conversation with Capt. Bull, asking him his opinion of the Disposition of the Allegeny Indians, concerning their delivering up the Prisoners. He thought it wo.d be difficult for them to resolve to deliver them all up. We cross'd Moshewatchowall & Nescopecs Creeks,[9] and were exceeding glad to find some grass for our Horses, on the Susquehannah Mountains, & tarried a while to refresh them & ourselves. Capt. Bull went before us to Waiomick [10] and we came there about Sunset. Teedyuscung had been gone about two Hours before our Arrival, but I found they had dispatch'd a Messenger after him, to bring him back, which he readily comply'd with. Here I found such obstacles had been imprudently laid in my Way, that I was troubled & grieved in such sort as to repent I had ever undertaken this Message.

[May] 12th. About Dinner Time Teedyuscung came back & was glad to see me. In the Afternoon he call'd all his Men together in order to hear what Message I had. I told him Bror., you know it is a Rule & Custom that Messengers do not tell their Message before they come to the Place they are Sent to; but as you are the Counselor & Agent for this Province & it is commanded by the Governor, that we shall conferr with each other abt. Every Thing, so I will hide nothing at all from you. I accordingly communicated every Thing to him, & he seem'd mightily pleas'd with every Thing, 'till I came to the Word [Relation][11] in the Generals Message. Said he: We sho.d first see to establish a firm Peace with them, there are many Nations that will come in & when they hear of threatning it will startle them & incline them to draw back instead of coming nigh. I think we sho.d be mild & loving untill we have gained them into our Interest. Then if they will not behave well we may take a Rod or Whip to chastise them with and bring them to Reason. We had much agreeable Conversation together till Midnight.

---

[9] Nescopeck Creek flows west into the North Branch of the Susquehanna River at the present-day Luzerne County village of Nescopeck. Donehoo (1928:127) translated the name to mean "black or deep still water." The name Moshewatchowall translates as "Bare Hills," the current name of the mountain ridge separating the Lehigh and Susquehanna drainages at this point. Post may have been referring to the mountains. If not, then the identity of a creek going by this name is not known.

[10] Wyoming "broad or great flats," the stretch of the North Branch of Susquehanna River around the present-day city of Wilkes-Barre, Pennsylvania.

[11] The word should read *retaliation*.

Sunday [May] 11th. Sett to the way Early and Arived at Wioming[3] in the Evening, Where we were Informed that Teedyuscung[4] was Set off on his Journey this Morning but they Sent for him Imediately on our comeing.

Monday [May] 12th. Teedyuscung Came home about Eleven oClock, and we had Several Conferences with Him this Day.

---

[3] See ff. 10, p. 40.
[4] Delaware chief Teedyuscung maintained his primary residence at Wyoming in a log-cabin town built at his request by Pennsylvania authorities in 1759. He continued to live at Wyoming until he burned to death in his cabin there in 1763.

Hardly any Thing of all the Goods, Horses, &c. that was distributedamong the Indians was now to be seen amongst them.

[May] 13th. We set about making the Belts, I exchanged White for Black Wampum. I had a Conference with Teedyuscung. He said: Br. I am glad God has spared your Life, because you have begun the good Work of peace at Allegeny, and when we have begun a good Work, or have Planted any Thing we must be carefull & see how it grows, else it will come to nothing at all. It is good also that we do our best that it may not remain under Ground. We then spoke a great deal abt. The first Agreemt. Which Onas[12] made with the Indians at his first coming into this Country, how he was Adopted & received into their Family as a Child. Further that it had been formerly agreed to by all ye. Nations that the Delaware Country sho.d never be incommoded with War, but always enjoy an undisturb'd Peace & Tranquility. I told them the reason of their Disturbance was, that you have left your Mother Country & joined yourselves to a Strange Nation, whom your Grandfathers knew not.[13] If you now all return you will again enjoy the same Peace your Grandfathers had. To which he answer'd: it is just as you have said. After which he desired me to read over the Treaty's & Messages of Governor Morris, wch. employ'd me the whole Day.

I wrote to Mr. Holland at Shomokin,[14] to acquaint him that it had been agreed on at the last Conference in Philadia. with the Indians, that Teedyuscungs Wife, during his absence sho.d be supply'd from Time to Time with Provisions & Necessaries from the Fort.

[May] 14th. It Rain'd all Day long, I conferr'd with Teedyuscung & urg'd him to loose no Time but set out as soon as possible. Two of our Company were Sick. The Belts for him and me were not yet finish'd, therefore he desired us to stay till the next Day & then we sho.d set off. He talk'd a great deal with me about the first breaking out of the War, how the [....'s] did publish it before it broke out & desired them to hold themselves in readyness, but, said he, we are no more inclin'd to be under their Influence, which he feared would in the end Occasion a War between them.

---

[12] A formal Indian term for the Governor of Pennsylvania, first given to William Penn. It is an Iroquois word for feather; Miquon is its Delaware equivalent.

[13] I.e., the French.

[14] Nathaniel Holland was the provincial agent at Shamokin, a major Indian settlement and site of the provincial outpost of Fort Augusta at the forks of the West and North Branches of the Susquehanna River at present-day Sunbury, Pennsylvania.

Tuesday, 1st, [May] [13th]. Wrought at Makeing Belts and Strings of our Wampum, was Used very Kindly and talked of Going Next Day.

Wed'y 14th. [of May] Very Rainy Wether so that we Could not set out, So we folowed our old Business of Belt making.

[May] 15th. Mr. Hays & Isaac Still went a fishing but catch'd little or nothing. We help'd to set up Teedyuscungs Fence. Teedyuscung instructed his people how to behave on the Road, that they should mutually assist each other in making Fire, fetching Wood, hunting up the Horses &c. & that when they had got something they should be careful to share it equally, & be sure to give me and Mr. Hays our Portions, for, said he, they are not used like us, we fall foul of every Thing like Wolves, but they are regular & have their stated Times for eating & Drinking, & so would come short, if not carefully provided for. To me Teedyuscung said: Br. Be strong, exert yourself in the Business you have undertaken keep to the Instructions you have received, & fear no Body; We will see that all Things shall come to rights, & if there remains any Thing unjust & rusty in them, where we are a going we will clean it & make it strait. Every Thing is very dear here, half a Pint Molasses 5/.. a lb Butter 2/6. a Quart Milk 8d. Rum 20/ a Pint.

[May] 16th We made all ready to set out, but just as we were going off there came a heavy Gust of Rain with Thunder & Lightning, which holding on discourag'd our Company from setting out. I had some close Conversation with Moses and Isaac Still & laid our Message & affair close to their Hearts & consideration, telling them the End & Intent of our being sent. Mr. Hays & I were employ'd almost the whole Day in making Strings. The Belts were finish'd & I paid 500.d black Wampum for making them. Two Women from beyond Atsenetsing[15] Arriv'd & brought us Word, that the Indians there were waiting for us, & desirous to see us, which very much encouraged Teedyuscung.

[May] 17th We arose early & hunted for our Horses, & with some difficulty we set off abt. 8 oClock. We took our Course E. By N. We cross'd ye Creek Weshachchapohg[16] & came to an Old Indian Town where only a single Family now lives. We pass'd by another Waste Town & Lechchowechlegs, where ye Mennissing Indians formerly liv'd.[17] We reach'd as far as Quetote-

---

[15] At present-day Corning, New York. See p. 8.

[16] Unknown.. Donehoo (1928:107) translates the name from Meshoppen "place of beads."

[17] The Lackawanna River. The Mennissing Indians were from Minisink, a major Munsee community above the Delaware Water Gap. Mostly hostile to the British at the beginning of the war, many had moved to the upper reaches of the Susquehanna Valley where Post and his party were headed.

Thursday, [May] 15th . Wether the Same, so that we wer Oblidged to Ly by as Before and Mad Belts.

Friday, [May] 16th. Designed Going, but Teedyuscung would not Go untill he had a field of Corn planted first, and we all assisted him and planted it this Day.

Satturdy, [May] 17th. Set of Early and traveled smartly crosed a Large Creek about one o'Clock called ahlahonie,[5] and so folowed Our course up the East Side of the Sisquhana River till Night, and Set up our tents in an Old Indian Town called Quelootama,[6] Being fourteen in Number, in all.

JOHN HAYS' DIARY, MAY 17 - JUNE 28, 1760

[May] 17th Seterdy we Set out[a] A Nore est corse A Bought 8 Miles we cr[ossed] Aleheiene[b] and Eate Our Diner an[d] Went a North corse till Night and Lodged in Quelotmoe[c] that Night 12 miles we had in Number 12 ind[ians] in compen[y]

---

[5] See ff, 15, p. 44.
[6] Quilutimunk or Wyolutimunk, in Lackawanna County near Ransom, Pennsylvania.

[a] From Wyoming.
[b] Lackawanna.
[c] See ff. 6, this page.

monk and Old Indian Town,[18] & there made our incampment. Our Company consisted of 14 Persons, 10 of whom were apointed to go to Allegeny. Fred. Post, King Teedyuscung, Capt. Jno. Bull, Amos,[19] Lieut. Hays, Capt. Moses Tattamy, Isaac Still, James, Chappe, Chechequait, or George & his Wife Chupotetis.

[May] 18th. Our Horses stray'd a great Way back again. I boild Coffee for Breakfast. Isaac Still in going down a very steep Hill fainted away. We dined at Sakapochkung.[20] At Dinner Teedyuscung spoke to ye. Company; Hearken Boys! It is not good as we have hitherto gone on, you have been too much out of the Way, we sho.d look more to him that made us, & ask his assistance, and then he will help us along on our Journey; Here we have one along with us who can tell us what is good, if we will listen to what he says! (pointing to me) We sho.d not live like the Beasts in the Woods &c. Observing his People did not much Mind what he said it gave him some concern. I meditated much on the Business I have in hand, desiring the Lord to lead guide & direct me in it & to Act with Mankind as he Acted with them when in the World, & walk with that Meek & lowly Spirit he was possess'd of. We cross'd thro' Tinckaneck[21] which is good land but uninhabited. It raind hard almost the whole Day. We came as far as the Sugar=Cabbins of Mamechtoshunck[22] where we took up our Quarters that Night. We were all wet to the Skin.

[May] 19th. We rose early & went to look for our Horses. A Man and a Boy came from Machaihosung, an Indian Town,[23] & refresh'd us all with Bears Flesh. After we had dried our Cloaths, we set off for the Town. Experience

---

[18] See ff. 6, p. 45.

[19] Amos was then Teedyuscung's eldest living son. He and his wife, Justina (a sister of Christian Post's second wife, who had died in 1751) were baptized by the Moravians on December 14, 1750. Believed to be 22 at the time of his baptism, he was probably 32 at the time of his journey to Secaughcung.

[20] Unidentified.

[21] The word translates as "little creek." Post refers to the present-day Lackawanna County city of Tunkhannock where Tunkhannock Creek flows into the North Branch of the Susquehanna River.

[22] Not otherwise identified.

[23] In the present-day Bradford County city of Wyalusing.

Sunday, [May] 18th. Wet Wether, Nevertheless, we traveled Smartly Cross a very Large Creek called Washcoking,[7] Lodged on the Banks of Sisquhana, and had A .Very Wet Night of it.

Monday, [May] 19th. Set of Early, tho wet, and Arived at a town called Quihaloosing,[8] the Governours Name Wampoonham,[9] a Very Religous Civilized man in his own way, and Shewed us a great Deal of Kindness, and we held a Conference with him this Evening, and when over Mr. Post Gave us a sermon at their Request.

[May] 18 Sundy Moring we Treviled and had A wat Day and came to Tinguanet abt 13 miles and came to A Nother crice cal[led] Weshaking[d] we came A Bough[t] 30 Miles that Day

[May] 19 Mondy Weat in the Mornin[g] we Set of and came to a Tow[n] caled Mochailucen[e] A Bought Three A clock and Piched our Tents and Eat Diner Our Cook was Neaxty and Maid Very Bad Brot[h] For ous I could Not Joene With then ~~And~~ That is A Pout Ten Miles ~~10 Miles~~ we held A confrances that Night and had Prayers by Mis Poist[f] that Nig[ht]

[7]Meshoppen Creek.

[8] See ff. 22, p. 46.

[9]*Papoonan*, also known as *John Papunhang*, a Delaware religious leader who settled at Wyalusing with his followers from 1758. Joining the Moravian brethren in 1763, he and his people moved to the Moravian mission of Schoenbrunn in New Philadelphia, Ohio in 1772. He died there in 1775.

[d] Tinguamet is Tunkhannock (see ff. 20, p. 46); for Weshaking, see ff. 7, this page.

[e] See ff. 8, this page.

[f] Mr. Post.

daily shews me, that God manifests his Power in my Weakness. My Health is but very indifferent, sometimes I think I must give out, & that it is impossible for me to git along, but then again I turn my Eyes from my self & look up to my gracious God, who renews my Strength. About Noon we came to Machachlosung, which in the Indian Tongue signifieth an Old Man. The People we found all at Work in the Woods, they are an industrious People. They begun this Place abt. 2 Years ago & now it is a large Town, and according to ye Indian Way fine Houses. They are Religiously inclin'd, & by no Means allow of drinking Rum. Their Religion chiefly consists in strictly adhering to the ancient Customs & Manners of their Forefathers, thinking it is pleasing to God that they strictly observe & keep the same, on which Account they are much afraid of being seduced and brot. off from their Ways by the White People, from whom they will receive no instruction.

We staid here the whole Day & the Inhabitants were very kind & civil to us. Abt. 8 oClock 4 Indians arrived from Atsenetsing. The whole Towns People came together & Teedyuscung, by a String, acquainted them of the Message we were charged with, & shewed them the Belts both of the Governor, & the Indians with which he was intrusted. He also inform'd them of what the Governor had said concerning the Prisoners. The People here knowing me well desired much that I would keep a Meeting for them, which I comply'd with. My Text was: "Peace be unto you." They were all to a Man very Attentive, & I believe what they have heard will not be without a Blessing to them. They afterwards came & thanked me much for my Discourse & staid with me till Midnight. There was about a Hundred of them.

[May] 20th We got up early & fetch'd our Horses. The People in the Town made Breakfast for us. They met & conferr'd together & afterwards sent for us. Their Head man [24] spoke as follows:

"Brother! Hearken to what I have to say!"

I heard you Yesterday; you desired I should go along with you, to see how the Work of Peace goes. I heard and understood you well. But now I'll let you know that I am weak & Poor & cannot go. It is enough if you go, & whatever you agree upon Let me know, & when I hear of any good Thing I'll lay hold on it and will assist in strengthning it, as far as I am able." Giveth 4 Strings

"Brother! Listen to what I am going to say.

---

[24] See ff. 9, p. 47.

48

Tuesday [May] 20th. They Called us to Council and seemed to be very friendly and Delivered to Teedyuscung three prisoners By a string, and promised to bring them Soon down; this town is Situated on Sisquhana, East side about twenty Houses full of People, Very Good Land and Good Indian Buildings, all New; had Sermon this Evining again.

[May] 20 Tustey We were cald to A confrance and the Seemed in A very Good Dispesion fo[r] Pease and Very cind and Give us [ ] of Provsion in A mesort o[ ] Bene cakes and [ ] [ ]e Heald two or thre confrances [ ] Them and the Deliverd to the King[g] [3] Prisener In trelys But I have Not Sen them yet the Towne Stanes in A fine Place and they hav fine Buldings and Lives very Well and have Plenty of Corn and A Fine Place of Land And there is About Sixty in Counsil of Men Which Seemed Very Relidges Peing Desires to hae Mr Poist ot Spak ø to them This Night we Saw the Prisners and there was two Presented and they Said they had A Nother that was Not at home that Would come With them two one Litele Girel Named Yonica Vanata from Alinick[h] & another Mary frome mincg[i] Tulphaking[j] & A litel Boy Name was John His Parents Not None by us But they had one that they Would Not Let us hav it but they Say he Must give it up if he Will Liv in their Town

[g] Teedyuscung.

[h] Allegheny.

[i] Minisink, on the upper Delaware River at the border of New Jersey, New York, and Pennsylvania.

[j] The Tulpehocken Valley around present-day Reading, Pennsylvania. The name means "Turtle place."

Post Journal, May 20 *continued*

Last Fall when you pass'd by here I heard what you & your Brn. the English have agreed on, I rejoiced to hear you; that was the Reason I delivered up the Horses, that were brot. here from the White Inhabitants when you came back. Look Brother, listen to what I have to say. We heard you last Night; you told us what our Brn. the English have so much at Heart & what they desire. We all let you know, that their request, concerning their own Flesh & Blood, shall be granted. We are assured that God knows & sees us as we are, we have not been honest, we have been false & Hypocrites, in so long detaining your Flesh & Blood, & yet at the same Time we thought to please God.

"Bro. Now we will tell you, all those who belong to this Town or Society, have no more than 3 Prisoners, which we will deliver up to you, for we desire to do Justice & love God. Bror. We cant' however command others, that are lately come here to live, that they deliver up their Prisoners, Bror.! Now I will freely do what my Brethren the English desire of me; and I wish it was in my Power, I wo.d git back all the Prisoners that are every where scattered about in the Woods."

A String

Afterwards we council'd together amongst ourselves, to return them Thanks for their Sincerity & good Disposition. After they had been call'd together, I spoke to them as follow's:

"Brethren! Listen to what I am going to say,

in Behalf of our great King, Onas, the Governor & all the Inhabitants of Pensylvania. I have the Pleasure to acquaint you that our great King has no desire to go to War against any Indian Nation whatsoever, & that he has been thoroughly inform'd of all the Transactions between the Indians & his Subjects. He, as a tender Father over all his Children & Allies, was much pleased to hear of your Disposition towards Peace. And he has commanded all his Generals & Governors to use their best endeavours to establish a lasting Peace with all the Indian Nations, on a more firm Foundation than ever, durable as the Mountains & to last as long as Sun & Moon give Light. The which all our Generals & Governors have engaged & joined to perform as much as in them lies. Brn., You know it is a great Joy to a Mother to hear of her lost Child; it is now such a Joy to me, to find you in such a good Disposition, that you are willing to restore our Flesh & Blood. Brethren, I desire you to be strong & to hold fast the Peace offer'd to you. I know it will rejoice our Peoples Hearts as well as my own. I now thank you in Behalf of Onas, the Governor & all the Inhabitants of Pensylvania. And I by this String assure you of their good Disposition & Love towards you."

At the Conclusion of this Speech, the Prisoners were brought in &

Post Journal, May 20 continued

presented to us, Namely, A Boy, his Name is Jacob, from Tulpehocken,[25] was brot. to this Town from Allegeny. A Girl Janetje, was taken from the Menissinks a Daughter of Peter Van Etten.[26] A Young Woman, named Mary, born in Bedford in New England, but they co.d not tell me where She had been taken.

In the Evening we met again, when they gave me the following Speech:

"Brother! listen to what I am going to say! I am great rejoiced at that good Peace which is so well establish'd, & we all heartily join to it, we like to live in Peace. Bror. I beg you will have Pitty on us, & give no Strong Liquor at all. We that live here at Machachlosung, we beg; that if you sho.d see any of our Young men, who upon asking tell you, they come from Machachlosung, then pray pitty us & give them not a drop of Liquor."

4 Strings of Wampum

After this at their desire I kept them another blessed Meeting, & so ended this Day happily & retir'd to our Tent to rest.

---

[25] See ff. j, p. 49.

[26] Descendants of Peter van Etten still live in and around present-day Port Jervis, New York.

[May] 21st Arose at Day-Break. I was busily employ'd in finishing the Writings &c. Then they met again and we repeated to them the Yesterdays Speeches, & I deliver'd the Letters, I had wrote for them to his Hon: the Governor. They then beg'd I should tell them once more some Words about their Creator, for they were hungry after it, that so they might remember it after I was gone. This I did & so we took hearty Leave of them & cross'd ye Machachlosung. Six Miles from thence three Indians from Atsenetsing overtook us, who said Brn., we must tell you, we have some bad News amongst us, we would say nothing about it in that Town, because those People do not like to hear of War, and you spoke Yesterday of that great God who made us. They told us a very long Story concerning which I intend to inform myself when I come to the Place where it was propogated. We dined at Mesakachkung[27] & came that Night to Wesachsing[28] & encamp'd. They had kill'd a Deer & refreshed us with the Meat.

---

[27] Not identified.

[28] The present-day Bradford County village of Wysox. Donehoo (1928:263) translates it as "rush or bog meadow." It more properly comes from Wisawsing, "yellow place."

Wednsday, [May] 21st. They told us there was another prisnor in this town, but the man that had hir would not Consent to Give hir Up yet, but if he Did not he Should Leave their town; We Set off about Eleven o'Clock, and Crossed Quihaloosing Creek about a mile above the town, shortly after there Came four Indians after us and told there was bad News where we were Going for one of their Indians; being out a hunting had Spied a fire and Coming up to it there he found an Indian Lying asleep; as he thought, covered up with his Matchcoat,[10] and he presumed it was none of their people, Seeing a French Ketle'[11] and so was Going off when the Sleeper Awoke, and Spying him, waved his hand to him as tho he wanted to Speake with him, But when he Came Back he Could not Understand him, nor the other him, but takeing the Delawar Gun to Look at it, as he thought, Shot the Delaware through the arm, and broke it, when the Delaware Ran away and Escaped, tho hard pursued for a great way; then we Loaded all with bullets, and the

[May] 21 Wendy A Bout 11 A clock we Set of and When we had Gone A Bout A Mile or two there came fore Inding After us And Said that there wase Bade Nues Were we were Going and 6 Day A Go [th]er wase one of thire Indeings [wen]t out to hunt and he Sawe A Fier and A Indening Lying at it he prsived And a Mane He Wase None of their Papel for h[e] had A Frensh catel And he woak and weaved His hand and would have him to come to him and Wen he came he Tuk his Gune and Looked at it and at Last Shot at hime Brok his arme and he Rine A way and Got home and they has Sume Discurs But cold Not onder Stand Each other But he Said he wase Lost and That there wase Six in compiney and they are Very much A feard of ware and We All Loded With Baule for wa[   ] We went A North corse A Bought 14 Miles Very Bad Roade and Lodged On the River Got Sume Vinison and The Seemed All A fraid of ware

---

[10] Literally, a coat made of thick fire-resistant wool originally worn when operating match-locks ignited by long fire-lit fuses known as matches. Although matchlocks were no longer used after the 17th century, durable match-coats remained popular among Indian people throughout the east.

[11] A French kettle.

[May] 22nd. If all those Stories, that the Indians have told us sho.d prove true, then I am sure it will not only be dangerous, but impossible for us to come thro' at all.

About Noon we reach'd Diaogo,[29] & with great difficulty we cross'd the River with our Baggage, there being only one little Canoe in which one Person at a Time co.d go over. Our Horses we Swam Thro', but were afraid to let them loose, the Water running so swift that it brot. them a great Way down the River. We had a great deal of Conversation with the People in this Place, they confirm to us that which we heard on the Road. We agreed to send a Message to the Indians who live up the River to call the Nanticokes, Menissings, & Mohickons, [30] to meet us at Atsenetsing. Teedyuscung invited them by a String of Wampum. We pass'd the Narrows & over a high Ridge which has a fine Prospect & Situation, & came to as far as Aschkokuckwawalochtet (which Signifieth a hole where the Snakes harbour)[31] where we encamp'd that Night.

---

[29] The town of Tioga where the Chemung River flows into the North Branch of the Susquehanna River at present-day Athens, Pa. Donehoo (1928:226-28) states that the name means "at the forks" in the Mohawk language. A major Indian town dominating a major approach to the Iroquois heartland within what was then the Mohawk sphere of influence, it numbered many Mohawk and Oneida families among its' heterogeneous population.

[30] Most of these people lived farther up the North Branch of the Susquehanna River at Chenango (modern Binghamton, New York), Ochquaga (New Windsor, New York), and other locales.

[31] Otherwise unidentified.

Indians seemed Exceedingly Afraid; We traveled Through Swamps, Rocks and Mountains, about 15 Miles, then came to the River, and took up Lodgeing on the Bank.

Thursay, [May] 22d. Set out Early and Came to Diahoga,[12] & Crosed the East Branch[13] about 2 o'Clock, Teedyuscung had a Conference with the Cheifes and Sent Some Strings up the East Branch to the cheifes to meet us at Asinsans and Set of Imediately and went about 6 miles and Set up our Camp at Snake hole.[14]

[May] 22 Thirsday Mornig we had Tea till Bracfast and we and we Went A Bought 14 Miles a and crosed Tigoa River[k] A Bout two A cloce and had Sum take [with] A Chife and ther is Sum Litel Houses and Sent by the King to Gether them To Gether to hold councel in Sume of the Townes and we went A Bout 6 Mills that Night and We Lodg in Snake Hole .

---

[12] See ff. 28, p. 54.

[13] The North Branch of the Susquehanna.

[14] See ff. 30, p. 54.

[k] Now called the Chemung River.

[May] 23rd we arose early. I had a great deal of Conversation with Teedyuscung about the Ohio affairs. We cross'd Packtchackoneck (which signifieth a River good for Mills)[32] Our Companions are good Hunters, & it is well they are, for when the Victuals is dress'd they fall to like so many Wolves, & indeed if we had not been so well provided for we sho'd certainly have Starved on the Road. To Day we travell'd a great Way I was very giddy & my Head Acked much. We cross'd Appapech[33] & dined at Uchocke-chung.[34] After Dinner we pass'd by Wenshpochkechung, where French Margaret's live's,[35] without calling, then we came to Queanaskake,[36] where the People were glad of our arrival. They set before us what they had for our Refreshment.

One Cobus,[37] who formerly liv'd at Waiomick, brought us Milk, Butter & Molosses to eat, who told us that there were a great Number of Indians together at Atsingnetsing to revive an Old quarterly Meeting which had been many Years laid aside, in which they related to each other their Dreams and Revelations every one had from his Infancy, & what Strength & Power they had received thereby.

When we came to the Place we found it to be true, that between this Place Diaogo is the best Land on the Susquehannah. The Chief Man of Atsennetsing[38] produced a String which he had received Yesterday from the Mohaaks, & said: Bror. Yesterday we received 3 Strings from the Senecas, which was sent to them from the French Mohaaks at Canowago,[39] they told them; that 6 of the Senecas had been hunting round the Lakes & falling short of Powder they went to Montreal to be supply'd by their Father,[40] that

---

[32] Otherwise unidentified.

[33] Apolacon Creek, which enters the North Branch of the Susquehanna River near the Tioga County hamlet of Apalachin, New York. The name probably comes from the Delaware expression "whence the messenger returned" (Donehoo 1928:7).

[34] Otherwise unidentified.

[35] A niece of the well-known frontier diplomat Madame Montour, French Margaret and her people were living near present-day Elmira, New York in 1760.

[36] Also known as Cobus Town, several miles upriver from Elmira, near Big Flats, New York.

[37] Originally from the Delaware River. Cobus had moved to Queanskake from the Lackawanna Valley near Scranton, Pennsylvania.

[38] Where the Chemung River splits into its Cochocton and Tioga River branches, at present-day Corning, New York.

[39] The Catholic Indian mission of Caughnawaga near Montreal, Quebec, which was largely populated by Mohawk expatriates from New York.

[40] I.e., the French Governor.

Friday, [May] 23d. Set of Early and Arived at Asinsan in the Evening, there Stayed all night.

[May] [2]3 And Set of and came to cobes[l] Were we Got cine Usige and A Sumptes Diner & had Good Buter & Melk & Went on Our Jiurney & we Saw one Litel Prisner with A old Squa & we Saw Sume Sorts of Hill chimes[m] & arived at A Sinsan that Night A Norwest corse Abought 25 Miles

---

[l] See ff. 35, p. 56.

[m] Perhaps hill chimneys, in reference to cliffs on the south side of the Chemung River.

when they came there, they found to their surprise many 1000'ds of French & Indians, such a Multitude together as they had never before seen in one Place, & as their Father took no Notice of them, they said come Father sit down & let us talk together, but he replied, No I hate you because you are the Cause that I have lost Niagara.[41] Hearing this, & by the advice of the Indians there, they made off directly. On their Way back the Canowago Indians sent them a Message letting them know they were all dead Men, because the French and their Indians were determin'd to cut them and the English off, & desired that this Message sho.d go Day & Night as far as it co.d reach, to give them Warning & to be upon their Guard.

In this Neighbourhood one of their Young Men hath been Shot by a Strange Indian, but their Old Men take no Notice of it, on the Contrary they have given Orders that if any strange Indians should be seen in these Parts that none shall fire at them. On which account Teedyuscung is of opinion, that it is done in Consequence of an old prevailing Maxim amongst them; that when the Chiefs find they can no longer govern their Youngmen, they call in some of their Neighbouring Indians to kill some of them, & by that Means bring them to Reason. These and many such like Stories I have heard, which I do not think fit to note down, as the Indians have their own peculiar Policy in relating one Thing & at the same Time thinking & acting quite the reverse.

[May] 24th. It was a very fine Day, & about 9 o'Clock they began their grand Festival, which afforded us an opportunity of seeing their Stupid & Tragical way of Worship. Their Priests or Conjurers, with about 10 Women, went first into the Woods to paint themselves according to their different Characters, their whole Bodies were painted all over with various Colours, some with the Addition of Rattle Snakes, some with Squirrils, others with Trees Birds &c. Thus adorned, or rather disfigured, they came all in a Row into the Town singing as they went e.g. One of them began singing: "I saw two English Birds flying together in Love," which all the others repeated again 4 Times, after which they went in Procession 4 Times round the Meeting House & then turning their Faces toward Sun rise; hollowing; all together as long as they had any Breath; Then they shook Hands with one another & call'd all the People to enter the House with them, where they continued Walking, Singing & hollowing the whole Day & Night untill 6 oClock in the Morning, when a Certain Spirit came over them & many Wept Bitterly.

---

[41] The garrison of the French fortress at Niagara surrendered to a mixed British-American army on July 25, 1759.

Satturday, [May] 24th. Set a string to the Mingoes at Pacihsahcunk,[15] to Call them to Council, and staid for the Return; this Day the Indians Began to Sacrifice to their God, and Spent the Day in a very Odd manner, Howling and Danceing, Raveling[16] Like Wolves and Painted frightfull as Divels.

[May] 24 Seterdy the Were all in Gaged in A kind of worship and had Provided three vineson and Two Beares and the went out Fill the wodes and A Bout 10 Cl and came home A bout 11 or 12 Cloce and were Dresed Lik Pilgin [pagan] times and there wase 3 men and Two Wemen and 2 men & 2 Wemen and Two Men and they had Grat Bunches of Flours on there heades and was Striped and pinted Beyond Neater[n] Sume Had Grene Rodes in thir hands and Snaks and Birdes & wonder full things Pented on them All colers One mane was Rid & one Womean Black they came in A String and they were All Neked from the Belt up and Went Round the hou[se] and went in and Dansed on and they Went out Sum times and Looked Towardes the Sun Rising Very oftens and tinued Night and Day and ther Wase A Grat Dell of Strengers Indings that Never Saw the Lik be fore Sum Old Men they had Sent For the chifes but is Not com yet

---

[15] Paciksakunck, or Pasekachkung, is another term for Secaughcung. The town was also known as Kaniushty, Canisteo, and Board Town. The term Mingoes refers to expatriate Iroquois people then mostly living south and west of the League heartland in the Allegheny and Ohio river valleys.

[16] Reveling or ravening.

---

[n]Apparently "Painted beyond nature."

[May] 25th. In the Morning the whole Company came out & stood in a Row towards Sun-rise lifting up their Hands towards Heaven & hollow'd Six Times with all their Force, shook Hands with one another and then went to every House to wish them a joyful good Morning. They came to us also, wish'd us the same, gave us their Hands in Love & Friendship, and invited us to their Dinner. After all was over I spoke with Teedyuscung, telling him I thought it wo.d be good for us to conferr together, before the Indians, we had sent for, came, which he readily agreed to.

Sunday, [May] 25th. This Day our Messenger Returned without any Answer; the Indians went on in the Same Manner as Yesterday.

[May] 25 Sundy & they Sang [illegible] out of theire Mouth & A Bout one A cloce We were All invited in to Diner & we Sat till he° Shaked his Shell and Sung & Looked up and Danced A Great While and in his on way asked a Blesing and at Last he Give the chief A Porshion in his hand and A Dish Full to our king[p] and it Lay on the Skins that was on it and the Seven that wase Pented Got two Peses of Fleash and one cace of Bread and we went in and and eat our Diners and the Preast came in and Give Sum Litel pees of A Belt That was cot for that Bisness and Every one that Got or that and Sum got the Skines of the flesh Went out to Give thanks and they Looked to the Sun Rising and holoed With the Litel wampom in their hand and the Skines A Bout their Sholders our king Went From his Game of cards and came Back Played [illegible] the skines wase Given to the old Squas and they Had them A Bout thire Sholders and holoed Stoutly and There came A cage of Rum and Our king told his Young Men That they Should Not Drink But Bull[q] Did Not Here him and Went out and was out that Night

---

° Probably the "old Preast" mentioned in the June 2 entry.

[p] Teedyuscung.

[q] Captain Bull, Teedyuscung's son.

[May] 26th. This prov'd a hard Day to us. Two Casks of Rum having been brought to Town. Teedyuscung call'd all his People together, and desired them to consider the importance of the Errand they came about & what great Things they were Intrusted with, that they were not here to drink Rum but to do their Business. His Son who accompany'd me from Philadia., took no notice of it, but soon intoxicated himself, & brot. one Cask half full of Rum & set to his Father's Feet. Yet he wo.d not taste a drop of it, but order'd it to be directly taken away. Several Indians in their Drunkeness threaten'd to kill us, others to burn us alive &c. Our Landlord defended us as well as he could, & drove them 3 Times out of the House. However at last we were oblig'd to retreat into the Woods, where by Gods assistance & Protection we ended this dolorous Day in safety.

Monday, [May] 26th. The Indians Haveing Got Rum Got Drunk, all in General, Except some old men, and Teedyuscung Behaved well on this ocasion, for when his Sone[17] brought in the Kegg with Rum he would not taste it; we were very much Abused and Scolded by the Indians, and thretned Often to Rost[18] us.

[May] 26 Mondy A Bout Ten A Clock Bull came in With the ceage of Rum to his Father the king took not on Drope and Sent it out with Eameas' They were Dronk in Every corner We were As Still as Mis and quait Sume of them Wanted to have Rosted us for they Like as Maney Raiging Divels But he King would not drink And Sum of the chiefes would not Teast of the Rum or We would have had a Bad time of hit we Looked the cloce Very often and Woushed for Night which came the Rum Wase Out and they Got Quait A Gaen The Meschender came Back and told That they would Not com but we Weated for Sume Othre Mesches that was Not yet com we Sleped Well and Hoped that w might Never See the Like A Gean We had Sum Sport but Dorst not Lauf at it for it was So Strains A Thing

---

'Amos, Teedyuscung's eldest son. He and his wife, Justina (a sister of Christian Post's second wife, who had died in 1751) were baptized by the Moravians on December 14, 1750. Amos was believed to be 22 at the time of his baptism.

---

[17]Captain Bull.

[18] Roast.

[May] 27th. We received a Message from the Senecas, who told us that the Chiefs would not come hither, as Teedyuscung would pass thro' their Towns, they would then speak with him, & just as they were about to send off another Messenger, Shomoko Daniel[42] arrived here with bad News, telling us: that the Mingoes Saluted both him & us, & were glad that we were safe Arrived at Atsennetsing. Nevertheless they were surprised that Teedyuscung had brot. us so far up the Country without letting them first know of it, that therefore they wish'd us a Safe journey back again from whence we came, & warned us at the same Time not to be so hardy as to proceed any further or to venture to come to Sekachkung. They had also sent a Messenger further up, to tell them, that before this Messenger reach'd them, these two Messengers might possibly be roasted alive. They likewise let all the Indians on the Susquehannah know, that they sho.d not deliver up any of the Prisoners without their Knowledg & approbation. This Message displeased all the Indians here & they kept a Council abt. it all the Afternoon. Teedyuscung desired I would send a Message to the Mingoes. I told him our Message had been concluded upon at the great council at Philadelphia, for the Benefit of all the Indian Nations, & if I return without delivering my Message, an Inquiry will naturally be made, how it came to pass & by whose means it was prevented. Besides, as this Message came without Belt or String, I know not what Credit is to be given to it. I ask'd all present what they thought co.d be done in these Circumstances? Upon which they begun to consider it seriously. The Chief of this Place prepared a Belt to invite the Chiefs of Pasekachkung & Mingoes, but Teedyuscung resolv'd to wait yet two Days longer to see if the Nanticokes would come hither, if not he would go himself to the Mingoes & send me word again what to do.

They threatned very much in this Place on Account of ye Murder of the 4 People at Carlisle,[43] their Relations living here abouts. That Spirit which is gone out to perswade ye Nations to shed innocent Blood is not yet quite laid, they still breathe Threatnings & Slaughter. It is impossible to express what a

---

[42] Also known as Shamokin Daniel or Essoweyowallund. He was a Unami Delaware man who often carried messages from Indian communities to Philadelphia. Hostile to the English during this period, he later tried to sell Post to the French while accompanying him on a diplomatic errand to the Ohio in 1762.

[43] A reference to the wanton unprovoked murder of Delaware Doctor John, his wife, and two of their children the previous February. One of a series of murders of friendly Indians committed by Pennsylvania frontier settlers culminating in the massacres of the Paxton Boy riots of 1763-64 (Vaughan 1984).

Tuesday, [May] 27th. This Day, about one o'Clock, Daniel Benet[19] Came Down from the Mingos town, and told us that they Bid us Welcome to this town, but if we Came any farther they would Rost us in the fire, and that they Desired that none of the Nations on Sisquhana should Give their prisnors, it was their Orders that they shoud keep them and Bid us Go home the way we Came, and Come any farther; We held Council Imediately to Conclude what was best to be Don with the King and Cheifs present, and their Minds were that we Should Stay some time till they would See the Reasons, and Said they would Make them Come to Council and Give their Reasons; it was a time of Danger, But we trusted that God would Protect us and Direct us for the Best, Both as to our particular Sircumstances and Publick Good.

[May] 27 Tustudy this Day was A Day of ware Very Bad News A Bout one A Clock I went to a frolick of Ma ing of Tuncy & Dineal Benit[s] came Down from the Mingos town A Bout half A days Jorney of and Said they Bid us Welkom To this town But if we came an aney farder they Would Rost Us in the Fire and that they Desired that None of the Nations on Sischania[t] Shold Give up aney of the Prisners it was there orderes that they Shold keep them and Bid us Go home they wa[y] we cane and Not come any far[ther] And Councl was Held By the king And the chifes that was there and They thought it Best that we Would Stay Sume tim til we Need What was the Reason of it and the would mak them come to councel and know the Reason that we Must Now G Go hom the Evening was Very Dark But we staid hoping that God Would Preserve us out of their Hands and Derict us for the Best and the Publick Good.

---

[19] See ff. 41, p. 64.

[s] See ff. 41, p. 64.
[t] Susquehanna.

Person must go thro' who is so press'd in such Places, where the Devil has such great Power. God our Lord help us graciously thro' these Dark Corners.

[May] 28th. We were up by Day-Break. At Sun-rise the Old Teacher of this Place went from House to House & wish'd both Old & Young Peace & a Joyful good Morning & thank'd God, who had suffer'd them to behold the Light of ye Sun once more. Teedyuscung desir'd me to Write to his Honr. The Gover, as follows:

"Brother: in the beginning of the Treaty I told you, that you & the Mohaaks kept Council together, you pointed your Hands towards us Delawares, & never suffer'd us to come to your Council, to git knowledg of what you agreed upon, you both thought these Delawares are good for nothing, why sho.d we let them come to our Council. Therefore I do not know of your agreement which you have made with them, nor will I concern myself or take any Notice of it. I will press on to finish that good Work I have begun with the English. Now I will proceed on my Journey to Allegeny, to see that good Work of Peace begun there & I hope I shall see it, & I will do my utmost Endeavour to bring all those Nations to a firm Friendship with the English. I shall not turn my Eye or Ear to the evil Disposition of the Mohaaks." ("Therefore I think it proper you should go back & tell the Governor of it, altho' it is against our Will & agreement; but I hope you will not fail to bring that good & agreeable News to Allegeny in another Way, when you have first consulted with the Governor. For my part, when I agree to any Thing, I do not keep it for myself in secret, but I hold it up & hollow loud, that all may see & hear of that good Work I am about.")

"Brother! I have nothing to say to you & the Mohaaks & about your agreement. You have put Fred Post & Mr. Hays in my Bosom, as soon as I came to Atsennetsing the Mingoes took them out of my Bosom to roast them; therefore I don't know what to say to you both, for I know nothing of your Agreements, I can't take no Notice thereof, for you must agree with them Yourselves. I will tell all the Nations not to take any notice of this, because you & the Mingoes have always conferr'd together. Pray do not send for me when you consult together, & when you have any differences & disagreemts. with them, for I will not come & concern myself about it. I assure you when I come I shall always come with Peace & about some good Work. Bror. take no notice of the Mingoes what they say concerning the People that were killed, for they have no business at all to concern themselves about our Flesh & Blood, let them settle about their own Flesh & Blood. When I come back

Wed'y, [May] 28th. The Indians told us that Sr William Johnstone has Corespondence with the French;[20] some told us to Go home and Bury the Indians that were Kiled Near Carlisle,[21] or they would Come and Bury them them selves Soon. We took Teedyuscung out and Began to talk with him by himself concerning our having to turn back, he told us the Mingos and Governour Use to have Confrences by themselves and did not trouble him, but Said he was a fool & he would not have any part in their Diferences, and hoped that their Roguery would be found out now.

[May] 28 Wensdy Not Ebeny[u] they have[v] We herd that Sir Milliam Jonston Hase coriespond With the frensh and More thay are Mad A Bout The Inding that wase Killed over Siscuhano[w] they Bad us Go hom and Bery them or We will Go and Bery Them our Selves Soone I have Seene Since I came to this Place But 3 Presnirs one wase A Girel A bout 18 Yeres of Eage & A Nother But I Spoak to hir and She would Not Spak to Me I No Not from where She came from and I Saw A Boy of A Bout 14 Year old I Saw A Litel Girel A Bout 5 or 6 Years old I now Noting of hir name the Boys Name is Daniel Williames from Minesike[x] his Father was kild and his Mother is Gon up to Jonston H[e] Wase A Bout 14 years And we went out to A confrance with The king and Expect we Will Sone part and the King Said he Would have no part in the Difrance But would Let the Gov[e]roner and the Siniker[y] Debet it them Selvs for they Used to confer With Them and Not call me for you Both Used to Say that I was A Fool and Nod no thing But they that you will Soon see the Rougs

---

[20] This may refer to Johnson's 13-14 February, 1760 meeting with the Six Nations at his Mohawk Valley headquarters in which the Iroquois delegates reported that they had met in council with their pro-French countrymen.
[21] This probably represents a reference advising the Europeans to properly condole kinsfolk of Delaware John and his family, who were murdered by settlers near Carlisle, Pennsylvania in February, 1760.

---

[u] *Nota bene.*
[v] This sentence is incomplete.
[w] The aforementioned Delaware John.
[x] Minisink.
[y] Senecas, who evidently exercised greatest influence over the area.

from Allegeny I shall talk further about that affair, you have already cover'd them."[44]

Afterwards Teedyuscung call'd all the Headmen together & ask'd them if they wo.d obey the Mingoes or rather join that Peace which was offer'd? They then consulted together & answer' d:

"My sister![45] listen to what I say! I am but poor and do not know how to speak right; If I speak any Thing that is not right you will be so good & help me to rights & not take it amiss, for I want to say that which is really good. My Sister, I see you are Sorry for the bad News you have heard. I likewise am sorry, my Sister: I by this String take all the badness out of your Heart & Mind & throw it away, & I would have you take no Notice at all of it, but to press forward in that good Work of Peace without any delay & be Strong & see that it be well establish'd all over, for I heartily wish for the same."

I was glad the Evening came to my Relief, for by much thinking & considering this Day my Head grew very Weak and poor.

[May] 29th. It was a Rainy Day. The Chief of the Place brot. me a Dish of Milk. I wrote the following Message to the Mohaaks.

"Brother! I hop'd to have had the Pleasure to see you with my own Eyes & to hear you with my own Ears, but I was quite surprised to hear from you, that you push'd me back & threaten'd to roast me. Bror., I'll let you know, that I don't come on my own account, No I come in the Name of our great King, Onas, the Generals Governors & all the Inhabitants, for a good Cause & for the Wellfare of you, your Children, & Grand-Children in Time to come, Brethren, I'll let you know that I can't give much Credit to such Reports as I have heard of you, for I know when Wise Men send Messengers they deliver their Messages by Strings or Belt. Brethren, you will remember that Peace was made & the Road clear'd thro' all the Nations, that Messengers of Peace might travel without Molestation & Danger; it is an unheard of Thing among Nations to threaten to Roast Messengers of Peace. I am no Child nor yet am I afraid of you; if you sho.d put your threatnings into execution, still our great King & Rulers live, & altho' he is a tender &

---

[44] Meaning the Pennsylvania government has already appropriately condoled Doctor John's relatives, thus removing the crime as a cause for retaliation.

[45] This is almost surely a variation on the use of the word "woman" used to address Delawares symbolically during this period. Even more interesting, this is the only example I know of in which Delawares address each other as "Sisters" when speaking to one another in council.

Thursday, [May] 29th. Waited for some Messages, but Came not.

[May] 29 Thurdy I Saw one Litel Girel A ~~be~~ Bout 7 or 8 Yeares of Eadg But I cannot Tell Name Nor Place Nor Wher She came from we Waited for Sum Mechsedges But they came Not We Lived Very Well For Vitels and Bede

Merciful Father to all his Children & Friends, yet he is nevertheless, a Mighty, Powerful, Wise & great King, has long & Strong Arms, & can reach the remotest Nations in the World to Punish whenever he pleases. Brother, I'll wait a while here untill I hear from you; What I shall tell our great Men about your refusing to let me pass thro'. I wish you to consider well what is to be done, for they now having sent me, will enquire into the reason of my coming back again: and what will the Allegeny Indians say when they hear of it. Brethren! I wish you may pitty your Women & Children, and let me soon hear from you that I may know what I have to do."

Teedyuscung desir'd of me, that, I should beg his Honour to let him have the Articles of Peace of the first treaty in Easton, concerning the great Peace Belt.

A Messenger came from Diaogo, who told us, that the Person we got had sent from thence to the Nanticokes had been 4 Days on his Way; that the Nanticokes was preparing to come, but just as they were about to set off a Messenger arriv'd from Onondago,[46] & that as soon as they had heard him they wo.d come.

We were all glad to hear from them, because we did not expect much good from them up the River. Isaac Still & some other Indians went to buy some Butter & Tobacco. A lb Butter 2/6. A lb Tobacco 20/-

I got a Message prepared to send to Allegeny, in Case they would not suffer me to pass.

[May] 30th After Breakfast I continued Writing. I gave Isaac Still my message to carry to the Mingoes. They Danc'd in our House till Midnight, which much disturb'd & broke our rest.

[May] 31st. Mr. Hay went out to shoot Pidgeons but got none. The Indians here, are much like the Polish Nobility, who mostly follow the Plough, yet feeding themselves with the vain Notion, that one Day or another the Crown may possibly devolve on them. So it is here, every one is his own King and Master, & altho' the Inhabitants in general are well inclin'd towards ye English, yet notwithstanding there are some base & Wicked Men amongst them who fill their Ears with Idle Tales. In regard to the Prisoners the Towns are gaping & staring at one another, I think, when such a Town Delivers up the Prisoners I will do so too, and none of them are concern'd to make a beginning. The Name of the Chief of this Town is Achkonachking, of the

---

[46] Onondaga, near Syracuse, New York, location of the great fire of the Iroquois League of Six Nations.

Friday, [May] 30th. We began to Make Ready Belts and Strings and Speeches wrote in a Large Hand that Isaac Still[22] might Read them. We Got word that the Meseager we Sent from Diahog is on foot, but no Answer from it. But we all waited for it; Teedyuscung Got my Gun, and Gave me a little fuzee[23] for it.

[May] 30 [Fidy] We Begune to mak Redy Belts and String for them to take with Them to Aligenia[z] that Isack Still might Read them to the[ ] We had to Draw it in Larg Riting So as he could Read it and we Herd that the Meshes that we Sent from Digoa is on fute but is Not com to us yet and we all Staid to here from it

I heard of A Prisner Girel Sister to Williames Name is Elisabeth[aa] A Most A Woman There was A old Dronk felo that Plaiged the king But When he was Sober he cam and give A Bout Two or three 100 hondred wampom for A trespas or Tribut for his Be hayer in Liker

I Give up my Gun to the King and he Give Me A Nothe gun

Sat'y [May] 31st. Waited without any Answer.

[May] 31 Seterdy Nothing But I Saw A Boy of A Bout 12 years No nam nor from wheare He came from but he wase With John fidler[bb] we had Good help and Plenty of Provsion

---

[22]Isaac Still, the New Jersey Delaware who, with Moses Tatamy and several others, accompanied the expedition as interpreter and intermediary.

[23]A fusee was a short-barreled smaller and lighter form of musket or rifle often favored by Indian hunters and warriors.

[z] Allegheny Country.

[aa]Elisabeth Williams and a brother named Henry were released more than two years later on August 19, 1762.

[bb]A memorandum in a much later portion of John Hays's diary not reproduced here mentions an Indian named "John Fitler or Hays."

Menissing Tribe;[47] The Name of his adjutant is Wejachkaposing, signifying a Pumpkin roast'd on one side.[48]

[June] 1st. Early in the Morning the Indians here all concluded to send a Message to Sachkachkung to compell the Unamoas by a String to come down.[49] They desired me to do the same to the Mingoes at Sachkachkung, as they themselves would have nothing to do with them. I told them I would send the Message I had already prepared for them. They said if I spoke my full mind at once they would not come. I said: Brethren, it is our Way to speak the plain Truth at once in full Terms in all we have to say, let them consider what they ought to do & Answer; and I am determin'd to Act in this Way, yea, & not to hide a single Thought from them I wish they may do the like. Isaac Still behaved a little Unmannerly, I therefore deliver'd my Speech, I had before Instructed him with, unto Moses Tattamy with Six Strings.

[June] 2nd. Teedyuscung said to me: Brother! The Things, for wch. we have been sent out for, lies near to my Heart, that a real Peace may be establish'd all over; I feel a Strength that you are with me & it gives me Courage, therefore I beg you will not take it amiss if I acquaint You of something wch. I think is good, I do not tell it to you by Way of Command, but that you may take it into consideration; I know very well that your Method is different from ours, we have agreed to be as one Man & to have but one Ear; I will cry very loud and strong when the Nations come, the Unamowas & Mahickons have bid me do so, & particularly, I will speak in strong Terms about the Prisoners: I don't speak because I want to be great, when I am alone I am very little in myself. I told him I was glad to see he was in such a Disposition,

---

[47] Also known as Eghohowin, he was a major Munsee leader who had represented his people at the 1758 Easton Treaty concluding peace between most Delaware communities east of the Allegheny country and the English. He later moved farther down river to the Susquehanna Valley town of Sheshequin in the present-day hamlet of the same name in Bradford County, Pennsylvania.

[48] Also known as Jachkapus and The Squash Cutter, he was a war leader of note who led the party that destroyed Gnadenhütten in 1755. He died of smallpox after surrendering himself to the English as a hostage to guarantee Indian observance of the treaty ending Pontiac's War in 1765.

[49] As the following passage shows, Sachkachking is another orthography for Secaughcung; the Unamoas are Unamis, whose ancestors lived along the lower reaches of the Delaware Valley.

June 1st. We sent a Mesuag with Moses Tamey, and Capt. Bull, Teedy-uscungs Son, to the Mingoes again.

June the first

[June] 1 Sundy we Sent A Miseig With Moses Tatemy Aan Bulle This is the Sekende Miseig that We have Sent and I heard from My Peopel By two Squa as and They wanted Me to help to Bild A hous But I would Not

Mon'y, [June] 2d. We were Diverted With a strang Storey that they told us of the Indians at Diahogoa' Seeing a Vision in the Moon on May the 29th, Viz., that they Saw 2 horses in the Moon, one Came from the East, the other from the West, and they fought a battle, and the Easterly horse prevailed and threw the other Down and fell a top of hin, and then Men apeared about one foot Long from the East and Drove all before them; the Indians were very Much Grieved at this Strange sight, and wanted to Know our opinions of it, but we thought best to say nothing about it. Moses and Bull Came Back in the Evening and Brought the Disagreeable Answer that we must Go back, and not proceed any farther, for they had Some bad people in ther Country, and they would not Come to us, for they Durst not trust us because of them that was Killed over Sisquhana.[24]

[June] 2 Mondy the old Preast Goes Round the houses Every Morning and Eveng Sayes Sum Sort of Prayers and he hase A Book of Pickters whish he Maid him Self and there is Heaven and Hell and Rum and Swan hak[cc] and Indiens and Ride Strokes for Rum and he would Read Like Mad of it in the Morning and Sing to the Sune Rising May the 29 at Digog the Peopel Saw A Straing Site in the Moon they Saw two horses In Batel and the one Next the Sun Set fell and the one Next Sun Riesing Preveled and they Saw Men falling on the horse that Fell Seemed A Bout A fote Long and it was Seene By the Hole Town Men and Wemen The Indines was Very Much Sore Prised and vexed and Axed of us What it Meaned We Lived quite and Lved A Indian Life and Had Plenty of hameney But We had No fleash Sinc the Cantico[dd] Tateme is come Back and Brings the Disegebel Newes that We Must Turn Bout and Not cary forder for the had Sum Bad

---

[24]Another reference to the murders of Delaware John and his family.

[cc]Swannock, white men.
[dd]Cantico, Indian dance

I assured him I had nothing against him, all what he had said I took in good Part. I desired him not to hide a single thought from me, that the whole Affair lay near to my Heart and I meditated much upon it, praying to God for his help and assistance, & to give into my Mind what would be most beneficial for the present as well as future Time.

A Messenger Arrived from Diaogo, informing us, that the People there had seen a Sign in the Moon on the 29 Ulto., to wit, that on Face of the Moon there appeared a Body of Men & a Horse standing by them, afterwards they saw another Horse comeing from the West, whom the Horse of the East run down, and all the People followed after.

Our Messenger came back from Sekochkung & told us that the Indians made excuses that they co.d not come to us, Pashanos[50] was already gone to Allegeny & they had sent by him all they had to say. Concerning my going to Allegeny, they let me know that it never was consented to by the 5 Nations that any White Man sho.d go that Road, that I had a great Kings Road by which I co.d carry Messages to Allegeny.

Bror. Said they, we have not said we would roast you, if you'll turn back, but we know there live many bad People further back, which would do it, therefore we advise you to turn back quietly; We do not say this of ourselves, but it to agree'd on by the 5 Nations, that White Men shall not travel this Way.

Teedyuscung was so vex'd & griev'd at it that he hardly knew what to do.

[June] 3rd. Early in the Morning we convers'd together seriously about these Matters. Teedyuscung said I am concern'd & my Heart is ready to break, to think that our undertaking sho.d be thus frustrated & as it were knok'd in the Head, I can't see how we can do without you. Moses said, he had had a great deal of talk with the Indians, they ask'd him why Teedyuscung wo.d have them together, for if he intended to speak with them concerning the Prisoners, they wish'd he might say nothing of them, for they wo.d not give them up, since many of their brave Warriors have died. Moses told them: then you break the Articles of Peace, & perhaps that may breed a War again. They answer'd that they did not care for that, they leave that over to

---

[50] Paxinosa, an influential Shawnee leader and diplomat. Born in Ohio, he was among the Shawnees who moved to Wyoming during King William's War (1689-97). Marrying a Delaware Christian convert, he was reputed to be a firm friend of the English. Paxinosa moved upriver from Wyoming to Tioga shortly after fighting broke out in the region in 1755. Relocating to Secaughcung in 1758, he finally returned to Ohio in 1760, where he died in 1761.

Peopel in that contry But Would Not com to us for they Dorst Not Trust us Becase of them that was kiled over Siskhania & the Nonty okes[ee] Was to com but they did Not com To To Pasikinking

Tuesday, [June] 3d. Delivered several Belts and String, and other things to Teedyuscung that we Could Spare, and that he had need of; in the Evening Robert Whites Son[25] Came with a Letter, and Belt and String, and Very Agreeable Speeches.

[June] 3 Tusty We had Plenty of Hominey But we had Now Bread Bull maid Cofey and we Eat hominey and Cofey to Gether and in the after Noon We had Teay the king Maid A keake of it We had Sum Buter Whit & Yelew and It Was Very Sweet and Good We Deliverd to the king Several Thing Was Making Ready for A Mearch & In the house Where we Lodged was the Gouerner and ~~Acka~~ his Nam is Achkonk Mincig Gouenarner[ff] and in the other End of the hous A capen[gg] and ~~and he had~~ He had A Borded Bedd and his Jornal on it and He was ~~16~~ 16 Times at the ware

---

[25]The son of Robert White (Wolahcremy or Ullauckquam). Robert White was the chief of Nanticoke people then living in the large multi-cultural Indian town of Chenango near present-day Binghamton, New York.

[ee]Nanticokes.

[ff] See ff. 46, p. 72.

[gg] See ff. 47, p. 72.

the Mingoes since they had forbid them. Most of the Prisoners are in ye Mingoes Towns. Moses told me, what a Capt. had privately told him, namely, that there was no Peace amongst them, but that they collect all their Warriors together in every Town keeping themselves in readiness, that if the English sho.d attempt to go further against the French, then to join them against the English, to fight them.

Towards Evening two Messengers came from Chenunge[51] from the Nanticokes & brot. me a Letter as follows:

"Dear Brethren. I will inform you that I cannot come to meet with you, all this Time I have not been well. I am sorry I can't come myself, but I send my Son & another Young Man with him. I am glad you are going to meet our Brethren the Indians, I hope the Indians & the English will be good Friends & live together as Bret.n. ought to do. We send our Service to you & wish you all well. The Lord bless you all. It is a Time of Health with us & so I remain your Brother Robert White[52]

This Message pleas'd every body here & so we concluded this Day.

[June] 4th. Early this Morning the Indians deliver'd their Message with 5 Belts & 4 Bunches of Strings. Two Belts came from the 7 Nations at Onondago, [53] to let Teedyuscung know that they joined in Peace with the English, desiring likewise that it might be establish'd with the Western Indians, in which they desired also to be included. This caus'd great reasonings amongst the Indians present, why they then wo.d not let them pass, & yet wo.d have Peace to be made. Teedyuscung shew'd great unwillingness to carry any Message from them, to the Wtern. Indians, for this reason, because they wo'd then boast that they had concluded the Peace between the English & them. Teedyuscung told me: Now Br. we will go further up to the Mingoes Town, & let them know this is the last Message from the English, & that they sho.d give an Answer if they wo.d have War or Peace. Then we broke up for this Time.

I spoke to Teedyuscung & told him ye Mingoes desir'd we sho.d send for Keckshetaw[54] or go to him, & that I thot. so too, but he answer'd: You have spoil'd the Mingoes, by giving them great Presents, that makes them proud & Lofty; if you English are afraid of thin, we Delawares are not.

---

[51] Chenango, at Binghamton, New York.

[52] See ff. 25, p. 75

[53] Either Post made an error here, or a seventh unidentified nation is implied.

[54] Probably the leader of the Unamis at Secaughcung. See below.

and had Taken 17 Prisners and there was one Women & the Reast had No heads on the Right hand and the Leaft A young capton[hh] and his Jurnel he has Been At ware 6 Times tok 4 two dead and 2 A Live

The Preast of the Town he keepes count of the Week for the Hole Toun and he Works 5 Days and Keepes the 6 Day and they way That he ceepes count he has A Litel Stick with 12 holes in it and He Putis ~~is~~ it up A hol Euery Morning and he Reades his Picter Book till Noon and then Gose to his Work A Gain

The Nanticok Chief Robert White Sent his Son with A Leater and Sayes he is Not Well and cold not com to See us but He Sent Sum Belts and Strings to the king and Spoake Well the Dansed All night

Wednsday, 3th. [June 4th]. We thought to Set homeward, but it Rained Very hard; they told us they wanted to have more talk before we Came away, with us; Young White and the King[26] had a long talk by themselves, and we waited for the Council Meeting and Shod our horses, Expecting to Go some Up and some Down; we were always alarmed with some Bad News they told us, of one of their women that was Killed at Albany.

[June] 4 Wensdy we thought to Set of but Reaned Very hard and they Said That they Would Meet and Go Heve Sume talk Before we Went A way and the king and White Had A Long talk in the Litel hous and we waited For the Town Meeting it cleared A Litel & ~~and~~ We Got All our horses Shod For to Go Sume ~~y~~ up and Sum Down for we lived in Sospence A Grait While and heard all Wise Sum Bad News we heard Of A Woman that was kild at Albeney and we Stay to See Sum Soart of A Seckerefisit Pig By

---

26. Teedyuscung.

hh Hays means that the captain had his bed on the right side, and the young captain had his on the left.

Towards Evening an Indian Messenger Arrived and inform'd the Indians, that the White People by Albany had kill'd an Indian Woman, & that General Johnson[55] by a String, had promis'd then that he wo.d endeavour to find out the Murderer & bring him to Punishment, desiring that the same Rule sho.d be observ'd by them also.

Afterwards I had some talk with Teedyuscung alone: I find that he is always jealous that his Honour & Character will be lessen'd by my bringing the Message to the Indians & that he wo.d much rather do the Business alone, than with any body else. We rested well to Night there being no noise among the Indians.

[June] 5th. About 10 oClock, all the People in the Town assembled together, when we acquainted them of the Messages we had received; Teedyuscung repeated the Messages which the Mingoes & other Nations had sent him & after he had done I spoke to them by a String.

"Brethren! I am exceeding glad I have this oportunity of seeing you together in your own Country, I bring you a hearty Salutation from Onas, the General Governor & all the Inhabitants & assure you of their hearty & sincere Disposition to make Peace. Brethren, they have all join'd their Hands together as one Man to do their utmost Endeavour to settle every Thing to your own Satisfaction. Brn. if you are upright & sincere in your own Hearts, it will be so, now it lies in your own Breasts. I desire you in the Name of all the great Men to be strong & sincere & lay hold of this great Work of Peace, as it will be for the good of you & your Children & Grand-Children after you. Brn. I desire you to pity your Young Men Women & Children, & be strong & see that no Time may be lost that this Peace may be finish'd soon, & well establish'd, on a sure Foundation.

Brn. One Thing I lay close to your Hearts, that is, concerning our Flesh & Blood among you, which we have so much at Heart that it disturbs our Sleep. Brn. let us honestly know your Disposition & what your Resolution in this Case is, speak openly from your Heart to us & keep nothing hid in your Breast. I confirm our true Love to you by these Strings, One is to the Munsees & one to the Nanticokes.

Afterwards I read to them the Paragraph out of the Easton Treaty, relating to the Delivering up the Prisoners. Then they all went to Dinner provided for them by Iawkaposin.[56]

After Dinner I wrote two Letters one to Sir Wm. Johnson for Teedy-

---

[55] Sir William Johnson.

[56] The above-mentioned Wejachkaposing, or Squash Cutter.

the chiefs of the Town Sum times we Expect to Go home and Sum times we Expect to Go With the king But that Seemes very Dengres for they Spak very Sose and Sum times we talk of Going A Road A crose the To the other Brench and By The Ketin Town[ii] and throw that was But we Do Not now What to Do the king Lead all the Belts out and there was Nine and 7 String and we Weated to here ~~and so far~~ and there wa[s] Nothing

Thursday, 5th. There was a great Sacrifice of a hogg which gathered a Great Number of them together, and after their Sacrificial Rites were Over they Encouraged us to Go on; But we Could not See it Clear, for the old father Mingo[27] always Sent us word not Go, but that Teedyuscung and his Indians Might Go, but that we should not Go, nor any White man Should pas through their Country, But being Unwiling to turn, and at the Request of Teedyuscung, who Was Desireous of our Company, We Designed to Go as far as Paseckachkunk, if possible.

[June] 5 Thursdy the capten that Lived in the house[jj] had A hog and would Make A Sort of Sacrifise And that hog must Be kiled & they kilead it in the Morning Be fore the Sun Rise and Brought it in and Lead With its head to the fire and its Tail to A Post and the Capton Sat and Sang half A Nour and they had Maid A fire out and they Singsed it and Boild it on the Same fire and Euery One that Did Eat they Got A Grain of coren the Hous was Swept and [the] fleash put in two Baskets in Smale Pesess and they Give A Pees to Euery One that Got the corn but he Song A Great Deel our king Recived and Gives all corn ~~and when~~ of his compney and we Got A pees of it and the head had A Stick Stopt in it
and the capton took it   and Song

---

[27] Possibly the Seneca leader Kinderunty. See below.

[ii] Kittanning, on the Allegheny River, reached from there by way of the West Branch of the Susquehanna River.
[jj] I.e., Wejachkaposing.

uscung, & one to Robt. White.

A Dark Spirit prevails here, with which the People seem to be possess'd: at our first coming here they roared against us like so many devouringLions, but when we set ourselves against them they seem'd to grow milder. How it will proceed further, Time will manifest, they opose both with Might & Subtilty, fearing to loose their Prey.

The Answer to Whites Letter I gave to his Son, & made a Present of some Medals amongst them; I explain'd the Signification; that it represented Onas's first coming into this Country, his establishing a durable Peace with the Indians, & that this Council Fire amongst us has never been quench'd to this Day, to which all the Indians can come & settle their affairs in Love & Peace: that his successors are still alive who continually keep up the same Fire, & that they might be assured Justice would be done them, & they might rely on their Love & Friendship.

[June] 6th We prepared to go further. I finished the Writings, but co.d not accomplish Yesterday by Reason of my Weakness. The two Nanticoke Messengers returned home.

The People have been all very kind to us. We took hearty Leave of them, they promised to follow us if the Weather prov'd fair. We pass'd by Kachkashehachkung where James Davis lives & they received us kindly, his Town is call'd Opashiskung & has abt. 10 Houses,[57] he will also follow us & see what Turn Affairs will take. The Menissings, Delawares, & Unamoas are quite displeased that the Mingoes have behaved so rudely towards us. It rain'd very hard this afternoon. We fix'd out Tent, & indeed I thank God we have such a Conveniency to shelter us from the Inclemency of the Weather.

---

[57] James Davis, or Awehela, was a Unami Delaware. He subsequently played a major role in founding the Moravian mission town at Sheshequin, where he was baptized on May 18, 1769. The Kachkashehachkung locale and James Davis's town of Opashiskung were situated at the confluence of the Tioga and Canisteo rivers. The name Opashiskung means "white clay place."

Round the fires and Set it Down to one of them and he Eate Sum and Gote up Agen and Sonung Round the fire and they All contico with him and he Set it to Another til 10 or 12 Had hit and When the Bones Was Picked they give them to the capton and he Rose Up and and went Round and Song as he Went and at Last he put them in the fire we put in the fire all the Bones we Eat and Bornt it all and Every one Rose and Went Rown the fire and Song and They Hole compeny Joyned in coras and the Elders went Rown With the Fat and they Did drink it and When they came to Me I Would Not and they all Laft they Eat it With out Salt For it up L ck Mad & they Went and Devided thre or for fadom of Wampm and Give it to them that did Dance and they Went out at The East Dore and Went Rown the hous Agenst the Sun and the capton first and they all Foloed Rouned to the Sun Rising and all haloed A Great While Sum Laft and Sum Look Mor Sad and they Song dreames of Sort of consration We were in coriged to Go on but it was But Dark for the old Rid cape chif Spoak A Genst us and Said that the King and The Indens Might Pas but that we Shold Not For no Whit Man Shold Pas that way Thruw thir contry but the king Would Go and See and he Was not A Feard

Friday, [June] 6th. We all Set of for Paseckachkunk, and Came James Davises[28] about noon and Dined with him plentifuly, but proceeded farther

28 See ff. 56, p. 80.

[June] 6 Fridy we Set of and came to James Daviss and he was Very Kind

[June] 7th. It continued raining the whole Night through. After Breakfast we proceeded on our Journey. We not 20 Indians going to the Place we last came from. We pass'd thro' Koshkosh,[58] where the Chief of the Mennissings lives there are 15 Houses. Three Miles from hence Labach Peter lives, in which Town there are 25 Houses.[59] This is the Place from whence the Wicked-one belcheth forth all the Lies & Suspicions dispersed among the Indians, which keeps them in continual Suspence & fear. We staid here about an Hour but co.d have no Satisfactory Discourse with them. We then went to the Place where old Nutimer lives,[60] they were very glad to see us. We gave him a Pair Stockings & a Stroud[61] & a Shirt in the Name of the Governor & Inhabitants of Pensylvania for which he was very thankfull. Teedyuscung rec'd an Invitation with a String of Wampum to come to Menokowak where Quetackon lives;[62] where we went & lodg'd in a New House just finish'd.

---

[58] Probably Goschkoshing, "Owl place." This town name recurs wherever Delawares or Munsees settled during this period. The precise location of this or the other towns mentioned by Post during this part of his journey up the Chemung River and its Canisteo tributary between Assinisink and Secaughcung are not known.

[59] Perhaps Peter, one of Teedyuscung's half-brothers. Peter was also known as Young Captain Harris, after their father, Captain Harris. Post's observation that Labach Peter's town was the place "whence the Wicked-one belcheth forth" conforms Young Captain Harris's known strong anti-English sentiments during this period. Noted as the influential chief of the Allegheny Valley Indian town of Venango in 1758, he may have been living along the Canisteo River at the time of Post's visit in 1760.

[60] Nutimus, the influential Delaware leader born in New Jersey who resisted removal of his people from the Lehigh Valley during the 1730s and 1740s.

[61] A length or blanket of stout stroudswater cloth.

[62] Also known as Kewetaickond, he was chief of the Unamis living at and around Secaughcung. First noted as a follower of Delaware king Alumapees at Shamokin twenty years earlier, he moved farther upriver when most of the Shamokin Delawares followed Alumpees' successor Tamaqua to Ohio in 1747. Menokowak is probably the name of the locality in Secaughcung where Quetackon made his home.

tho it Raind, Lodged on the bank of the West Branch,[29] in Woods.

Saturday, [June] 7th. Rained very hard, we Sent Bull[30] before us Early, we all followed, passed several Little Towns, arived at Paseckachkunk about four o'Clock after Crossing the River five times; this town Stand on the South side of the River, and is in two parts, at the space of a mile Distance, where ther is two Sorts of people; the Nearest part is peopled with Wonamies,[31] Quitigon[32] is their Cheif, the Uper part is Mingoes, which Commands all that Country. We halted at the Lower town, and in the Evening there Came nine or ten from the Mings Town, and Looked very Sower and Divilish, but went of after some time.

& we Got A Very Good Diner of Buter and Milk and we Went A bout 20 Miles A Nor west cors And it Rained we Lodged on the River Side[kk] and this Day we crosed A creek[ll] that Was Prity Larg Aout A Quarter of A Mile from the Town

[June] 7 Seterdy it Rained & we had cofey To Brexefast and Sum of them Set of and we all Set of and came by Two or three Touns and Saw two Prisners one was A man and the other A Litel Boy ~~We crosed~~ We went A Bout 15 Miles to Tekesakacunk[mm] Where were Arived At Three A cloce we crosed the River five Times it Stanes on the North Side of the River the River is very Smale Good Land And in the Evening there came From the Mohak Town A Bout A 12 of them & they Looked Like the Very Divel that wase the Town that they Said they Would Rost us If we came Theare and we Wery With in half A mile of it Now Bot they wetn of A Gen home

---

[29] The Canisteo River.

[30] Captain Bull.

[31] Unami Delawares, most of whom were descended from families who had been compelled to leave their former homes along the lower Delaware River and its tributaries.

[32] See ff. 61, p. 82.

[kk] Somewhere near Cameron Mills, New York.
[ll] Cochocton River.
[mm] The Lower Town at Passigachkunk, also called "little Passeeca," "Little Poosica," and "Litel Town Pasecakung."

[June] 8th The Chiefs of all the Towns here abouts met here, some of the Mingoes came likewise & behaved very rudely. Two Families came from Allegany & told us, that the Indians there were in a good understanding with the English, & that another Nation was Warring agt. ye Shawanos[63] & had Sculp'd some of their Wives & Children, of which they made complaint to the Delawares & desired help. Likewise, that they had been at Fort Pittsburg to make up all Differences with the English.

[June] 9th. They were all call'd together to a Council; There were present 24 Mingoes & Shawanos, there were of 7 different Nations.[64] The Muscochy[65] call themselves the Father of all the Nations,[66] some of their Chiefs I saw amongst the French at Fort DuQuesne,[67] their Cloaths were trim'd all over with Gold & Silver, & & one of them had a great Star on his Coat; they look'd very angry at me as if they wo.d have devour'd me. The whole Assembly consisted of 130 Persons. Teedyuscung inform'd them of our whole Message, I gave them a short account of the kind Disposition of our King, Chiefmen & whole English Nation, towards the Indians in general. At last they shew'd us civility & were pleased.

[June] 10th. They were the whole Day in Council each Nation seperately. I & my Companions met together, I address'd myself to Teedyuscung & said: Bror. We of the English Nation have done all in our Power to have Peace with the Indians, & I am persuaded no Nation in the World wo.d have done more; for my Part I can't see how any Thing co.d be done that has not already been done. I appeal to you if any Thing more co.d be done? They all answer'd they knew of nothing more. Therefore Bror., I tell you, now is your Time to speak your whole mind to them which he promis'd he would do.

---

[63] Shawnees.

[64] These may be the 7 Nations, perhaps consisting of the Mingoes, Senecas, Shawnees, Mesquakies (see next), Unamis, Munsees, and Mahikans, identified by Post as coming from "Onondago" in his June 4th entry.

[65] Almost certainly Mesquakie, more widely known as Fox Indians. They were a Central Algonquian speaking people forced from their homes in Illinois Country following a series of violent wars with the French and their Indian allies from 1710 to 1740 (Edmunds and Peyser 1993). Many Mesquakie expatriates lived among the Western Iroquois during this period. Today, many of their descendants live in Sauk-Fox communities in Oklahoma or on the Mesquakie Reservation in Tama, Iowa.

[66] As the Delawares were often symbolically referred to as Grandfathers.

[67] Post evidently saw these chiefs during one of his earlier diplomatic journeys to the Ohio country while it was still occupied by the French.

Sunday, [June] 8th. The Indians Gathered up from all the Little towns we had pased above Diahog, to See wt would be Don.

Monday, [June] 9th. This Day waited for the Council to Gather, and was Entertained at a Sacrifice of the first Deer a man had killed this Season; we sent for the Old Mingo father to Come to Council, and he Came and heard our Speeches, which pleased him, and promised Us an Answer tomorow.

Tuesday, [June] 10th. Got an Answer from him to this Efect, that he liked our Business and Called it a good work, But that we asked him a hard Qestion, that was whither we might Go through his Country or not; but we thought he had Sent a Message away to his Cheif and that he had Got no Answer as yet, so Could not Give us any.

[June] 8 Sundy the Indines Gathered ~~for~~ From All ye Litel Tounes Be Low To Council Whither we went or not Bak or foret So we wait

[June] 9 Mondy Like wise and there was A Sort of A Secrifies of A Deare they Boiled it All and Brought in the flesh When it was Boiled in A Basket and old Nutmegs[nn] was the oldest Man that was there and he came and Did eat his fill of it and the Broth was thick With Melk and He got the Skine on his Sholder And Went out and haloed and then the king Got up and Give To Every one and it was the first that Man had Killed in the Season Nutmegs Got the Skine Thanks and Biasing we Dined Sumptiously

[June] 10 Tusdey they Gathered from all Quarters I saw two Prisners One Wase A Boy about 18 yers old and A Girel of the Same Eadg But they Would Not Spak to me

---

[nn] See ff. 59, p. 82.

85

When the Chiefs & old Men were met, Teedyuscung spoke to them as followeth:

"Brethren! It is now about 4 Years since we begun to establish a Peace with our Brn. the English & I have laboured the whole Time to accomplish it amongst you. I now want to know your Resolution, for you have heard that the King, Generals & Governors, yea the whole English Nation desire to have Peace with all the Indians, I for my Part have made Peace with them & I will hold fast & firm to it. This is now the last Message & you can now chuse what you will. I confess I will have no fellowship or Part with those that will War against the English, but leave them to fight their own Battles."

This Speech made a great Stir among them, nor co.d they come to any Conclusion to Day. Many of their People on this account declared to their Chiefs, that in Case they wo.d not make Peace with the English, they wo.d leave them in Time & remove to the English & live among them, not doubting but they wo.d provide them with a Piece of Land to settle on. The Mingoes sent a Messenger to Kechzida & Pemetank,[68] where their Warriors live to let them know of our arrival & Message, inviting them to come hither & let them know their Resolution.

A Certain Fowl came flying over here from the Sea, to which a Mussel had fasten'd on the Foot, & drop'd down dead in the Place. The Meaning of this Phenomonon they took to be this; that they sho.d one Time or other drive the White People all into the Sea, I answer'd, if it had any Signification at all, it co.d not have that which they put upon it, for this Messenger drop'd down Dead in the Place, to shew, that if you will not have Peace, you are all Dead Men like this Bird. This Struck them all Mute at once.[69]

[June] 11th. They met all together again & gave their final Resolution which was:

"That inasmuch as you are come in the Name of the King, Generals & Governors, we cannot deferr any longer telling you, that we agree in this good Work & that we will help establish the Peace as well much as we can."

They gave 20 Belts & 13 Strings. The Chief of the Mennissings gave 6

---

[68] Probably the major Indian towns of Kuskuskies (along the Beaver River on the present-day Ohio-Pennsylvania border in Lawrence County) and Pymatuning (some 20 miles farther north in present-day Mercer County).

[69] Possibly because they recognized that their explanation was far more plausible than Post's.

Wed'y, [June] 11th. The Delawares and Wonamies and Muncies, held Council, and all aGreed on it, that we were to Go forward on our Journey, and Quitigon was to Go with us, But we must Stay Untill he would Get his New House covered; there was Rum in this town, But Teedyuscung would not Drink of it, nor Alow any of his Company to Drink, But when he was Invited to it said it was not to Drink, that he Came here but to do Greater Business.

[June] 11 Wensdy they held councel and All A Gread to it and then We wer to Go on our Jorney they Head Man of that Town Must Go along With us and we must Stay Till he Gets A New hous covered the cros Fellowes comes and Dances With the rest and Look pleased Be ~~Wat~~ What they Did we are not A Bout half A Days Jorney From they head of Sisquhaney They had Rim[oo] With in half A M Mile of us and the King[pp] Alow of Aney of his compney to Drink he Said he Did Not com here to Drink he came on Greater Bisness then to Drink Last night Thay Said that there wase Rum A coming and that he Shold joyn He said he would Not

---

[oo] Rum

[pp] The words *did not* should be inserted here.

Belts; All the Men & Women gave 13 Fatm.[70] Wampum & were all much rejoiced over this Resolution. They resolv'd that Unamoah[71] sho.d go along to Allegeny & that the Governor sho.d be inform'd of this whole Transaction. In the Evening they had a Peace Dance which continued all Night.

[June] 12th. This Morning they told me: "Br. you are able & we are poor, here is a Bull to be sold help us to buy it that we may eat together in Peace & Gladness." I readily granted this request, in the Name of the Governor & Inhabitants of Pensylvania, for which they thank'd me much. I wrote the following Letter, by direction of the Council & Teedyuscung unto his Honour the Governor.

"Brother, I let you know that we are arrived safe at Passekachkung, where all the River Indians met in Council, & all join'd in the Message of Peace which we deliver'd them for the King, Generals & Governors; and they gave 20 Belts & 13 Strings to join & Strengthen the same, besides which, the Men Women & Children laid together 13 fatm. Wampum, that the Peace may be firmly establish'd between the English & all the Indian Nations. Brother! I'll let you know, that they have solemnly ingaged & agreed to fulfil all the Engagements they have enter'd into. Brother, the Unamowa Nation had but one Prisoner & he was deliver'd up in Council, so they have clear'd themselves, & all the rest will follow their Example.

"Brother, I hope before I return from Allegeny the Prisoners will be brot. down. Bror. I hope before they come you will be prepared to receive them, they will come in August. In abt. 2 Days we shall set out from hence.

"The Mennissing Chief Annentammoakan & Quetaicund the Unamowa Chief, besides others, will go along to confirm what has been agreed on. Bror., I salute you & all the Gentlemen, & am your Brother

Teedyuscung

There arrived a Messenger who told us, that the Mingoes had taken 2 White People Prisoners & brot. Them off, but that they had been pursued, overtaken, the Prisoners rescued & two of the Indians were taken Prisoners.

---

[70] A reference to messages from the male and female inhabitants of the town rather than another expression of the Delaware ceremonial role of Women. See below. The 13 fathoms of Wampum total 78 feet in length.

[71] Almost certainly a reference identifying the Unami chief; see below.

Thursday, [June] 12th. We being in Want of Provision we bought a Bull, which Cost 1400 Wampum, and Rosted the flesh for our Journey; the Delawares and Muncies went off all away home, but before they went of they Lifted a Large Colection of Wampum for our Suport on the Journey.

[June] 12 Thirsdey we Bought A Bull and killed Him and Rosted the flesh for our Jorney he cost 3£-10S and the all Went home his Day and we Resolved to Work at guittiking is house[qq] and then We Will Go That Day When they All A Geed they Laid Down A Blanket and Preaclemed A Publick colection and for Joy the Wemen and Girels and children throd in wampom till There Wase 14 fathem for to helpe For Strings on our Jorney they Seemed Very Glead they Seem More Sivil [then] before

---

[qq] Quitigon's house.

That the Senecas had been inform'd of & told they sho.d come & see them but declined it. Some of the Onondagoes that were out upon a Scout fell in with a party of French, that the Captains of both Parties had conferr'd together, upon which the Onondagoes went home & held a Council together. I heard that they had kill'd an English Trader in the Town where Kecksheda[72] liveth.

Kewetaickond being building a House for himself desired us to help him to finish it before he goes on his Journey.

[June] 13th. Isaac Still & Mr. Hays went to look for ShingleTrees.[73] It is a hard Yoke, to have any Thing to do with these People, & what will be the End of them the Lord only knows, for Satan drives them to all Manner of Wickness to their own Destruction.

[June] 14th. I and Isaac Still went to make Shingles, & I work'd till I was ready to drop down. A Messenger arrived & brot. News that the French & Indians begun the Siege of Niagara on ye 11th Instant, It is abt. 3 Days Journey from hence.[74]

Another Messenger arrived & told us that 8 of their Chiefs would come here to Day.

---

[72] Probably Quitigon.

[73] One translation of the town's name, "Board Town," may refer to such construction materials. Modern Unami Delaware speaker Nora Thompson Dean suggested the name more probably derives from Sahkaxung, "Place at the side."

[74] This rumor was untrue.

Friday, [June] 13th. We went to work at Quitogons House, the Misquiteis Bit us so bad that I was Oblidged to Wrap my hankercheif about my face; there was none that stayed but Isaac Still and James Peepy[33] and me, for their young man went all away to the Other town and Got Drunk, so the work went Slowly on.

[June] 13 Fridey we Went out to Work and When we Began the Miscetes Bit So Bad that I wase obledged to Rap My hancerchf A Bout My Fase Bot the young Men Went ot the Town that was A Bove us and they Were All Drunk and here was None To work Isaik Still and Jamey[rr] & I and When we came home they Were all com to our Town and Going Like as Many Divels we left Post and Moses to Rost Sheare of the Bule and and they wer ferd A Nuf but Post Went out in they After Noon and Left Me to help Moses But the Rum was Soon Don and they Went to slep and the Work Went Slow the man kiled A hog for they frolick and the king took Two Drames and No Mor the wather was good I was Reding in the testiment and one of them Struck it out of my Hand and I was obledged to Quat I Durst Not Reead But sum times When they were in A Good Umer and Not Long at A tim

Saturday, [June] 14th. We Got word that the French had beseiged the English at the falls or Niagara, and that they were fighting now,[34] & that there was 7 or 8 Mohawk Kings on their Journey, and they Expected they would be with us this Night.

[June] 14 Seterday I Denied to work and I Went And Maid A Spoon And Mr Post Aan Isack Went to work then I Resolved that Would Not Dow Then I Went out & Said that I Would Work But there was Nobody to Take care of thing at Home and I would

[33]James Peepy was another New Jersey Delaware accompanying the mission as interpreter and intermediary.
[34]See ff. 73, p. 90.

[rr] Isaac Still and James Peepy.

[June] 15th. We conferr'd together about the Mingoe Chiefs that were expected, & I resolv'd to say nothing untill they gave me an oportunity to speak. The Captain from Paquiakinck came with Seven more, his Name is Wopenchachy[75] there came 30 in all to us, in a friendly Manner. The Capt. Spoke as follows: "Cousin! I have heard of your coming here with our Brn. the English & for that Reason I came to see you. You came to a dark Place[76] unto us, quite unexpected, it is dangerous where you came, I am glad to see that you came so safe thro', you have already spoken with our Father, Meskosky,[77] I wo.d be glad to hear what you have to say & what you are about."

Teedyuscung replied I have already said what I have to say, however, I'll shew you what I have to say. Isaac Still then spread the Belts 23 in Number: Teedyuscung spoke first of the Message which was sent to him from the 7 United Nations of Onondago, & then Isaac Still told them in Short, of the 3 Belts from ye Government & concerning the Prisoners. Wopenchaky said: Br. what I hear from you pleases me & I am glad I have heard you & I rejoice to see my Cousins, to Morrow I shall answer you altho' there are some hard Questions put to us. Then they took Leave of us & went Home.

---

[75] This is the above-mentioned chief Unami warrior at Secaughcung also known as The Squash Cutter.

[76] Perhaps he meant "from a dark Place."

[77] See ff. 64, p. 84.

Sunday, [June] 15th. Instead of the 7 or 8 Kings, there was 2 Captains[35] and a few Cheifs of Councilers Came; they Held a Confrence with us, the King[36] told them his Business and they took it to a Consideration, and so parted with us freindly, but Reconed[37] it Very Hard to Grant us Liberty to Go throw their Country, and Likewise to Demand our people that they had prisnors, for there was an old agreement that no white man Should pas throw their Country for fear of Spyes to See their Land.

[June] 15 Sundy and in the Efternoon they Said that ye would come & when they came there But one capton with Sum chiefs and they came and held A confrance With the king We did Not Know Whither they would Send us Back or Not For we were onder there orders for we Must Go throw their contry if we Go to Aligeney But they Seemed To come Lik men and not Lik the others That came first from that Town But When they heard Sum of they Speeches they Said Sum of they Requists Was very[tt] but to Moro the would Give A Nancer that was A Bout The Prisners and ot Let us Pass thrw For they Would Let No whit man Go throw thire contry by Sum old A Greement A Mongst them Selves For feer of Spies to See the Land this

---

[35] War leaders.
[36] Teedyuscung.
[37] Reckoned.

[ss] Shingles or clapboards, from which the town may have derived its' Delaware name, which translates as "Board Town."
[tt] The word hard should be inserted here.

[June] 16th In regard to the Diet & Way of Life it is difficult for White People to come thro' among ye Indians. Sometimes for Days together they have nothing at all to eat, & at other Times it is poured in upon them plentiful from all Quarters, then they are used to eat so much that they can fast again for many Days; A Mans whole Nature must undergo a total Change before he can get accostom'd to such a way of Life.

In the afternoon thirty Indians from the upper Towns came to give us their answer.

Wopenchachko shew'd a String that had been sent from the Dellowmatenos,[78] who inform'd them, that many Scouts were gone out against them & the English, of the Chippoaws,[79] that they had been at Fort Pitsburg & had cut off the Ears of the White People.[80] I myself have been two Mo. ago at Dellowmatenos & already kindled a Fire there & am ready to go there again. So that it is needless as well as Dangerous for you to go there. He also spoke to Teedyuscung pretty much in the same strain. Then turning himself to me, he spoke by a Belt in the Name of the 5 Nations.[81]

"Brother! I desire you to listen to me what I am going to say; I assure you I feel Pain in my Heart about your going this Journey, because you are placed in the Bosom of Teedyuscung; however I am glad you have put your hands to the great Work of Peace, to which we the 5 United Nations have also put our Hands. Bror. you did well that you put your Hand to that great work of Peace, but I feel sorry in my Heart that you are placed in the Bosom of Teedyuscung for we the 5 Nations tell you it will be a hurt for us & the Delawares if you proceed further. Now, Bror. we desire you pitty the 5 Nations & the Delawares, & do not proceed further a storm may possibly arise break off the limb of a Tree & knock out your Brains.[82] Bror. We thank

---

[78] The Delaware term for Wyandots, meaning "coming out of a mountain or cave." Then closely allied with the French and regularly supplied from their post at nearby Detroit, Wyandot towns mainly centered around the modern-day city of Sandusky, Ohio at the western end of Lake Erie (Tanner 1987:Map 9).

[79] Chippewas, also known as Ojibwas, whose communities extended throughout the lower Great Lakes north and west of Iroquoia.

[80] A metaphor meaning they had killed White people.

[81] Although the Iroquois Confederacy had consisted of six nations following the incorporation of the Tuscaroras by 1722, they frequently were identified, and identified themselves, as the Five Nations throughout the eighteenth century.

[82] Aside from being a thinly veiled threat, this statement also acknowledges that neither the Delawares nor the Iroquois could guarantee Post's or Hays' safety in communities that had so recently openly expressed extreme hostility to British occupation in Ohio Country.

day I Saw a Prisner Girell [She was A Doutor of Jacab Bayres] of About 9 or 10 years old that ~~eal~~ came with A old Squa that came From the Town A Bove and She Brought A Basket full of Shuger and Bred ot us And I heard of A women that came From Aligeney they Say that She Wase wife to one Miler that Lived Sum where Back over Sischeanea and there was About 30 in compiny With the capton

Mon'y, [June] 16th. We Got our final Answer to Go home, and they were Sory that we were in Teeduscungs Bosom, for they Said they feared it would be bad for them, and the Delawares on Sisquhana, for perhaps ther would Rise a storm, and the Limbs would fall and Knock our Brains out, and they and the Delawares would be Sorry for it, Lest they Should be Blamed for it, and that they Had begun a good Work of peace themselves and was Going to Alegeny soon to Confirm it; But was positive in their Answer that we must Go home, but Mr. Post Insisted Upon a Reason and a Liberty to Speake further Upon it, which they alowed, and Invited him to Come up to the Mingo part of the town Next Day and they would Hear him.

[June] 16 Mundy Now we waited for our Sentens Which they Soon Give to Go home fore they Were Sory that we Were in the Kings Bosem for they Said that it would Be Bad for [thim] the Mohakes and for the Delewarers For they Said that If we went on Our Jorney that Porhapes there Would Rise A Storm and that The Limes Might Breck and fall and knock out our Breanes and they weWould be Sory for they Would be Bleamed for it and the Doliwares and that they had Be Gun A Good Work of Peas them Selves and That they were going Back Soon to Alegeney to confirm it But they Said that we must Go home A Gene But the King Said that he Would Go up the Morow and Spak to Them and I Saw one Boy A Prisner that came from that Town and the capten Spoak Very Coragesly and With Great corage and they Went Home that Night and So ~~Mr~~ Mr Post Would Spak to them To Morow

you that you have put your hand to the great Work of Peace. We have done the same. I go now to the Dellamattinos, I do not know how it will turn out, but when I come back I will let you know as well as if you had been there yourself.

"Bror. I desire you that you would go Home quietly & I wish you well with all my Heart.

We reply'd: We have heard you, & tomorrow we will come to your Town & give you an Answer.

[June] 17th. Abt. 12 oClock we went to Pasekachkung, on the Road we met with a Shawano Indian half Drunk, the same that Kill'd Mr. Kroker at Waiomick.[83] He scolded & said: he never more wo.d love the English, & in passing by with a Hickory Stick, he struck Mr. Hays across his Back that the Blood gush'd out, & then rid away full gallop. Mr. Hays said, he never in his Life before felt such a Stroke.

When we came thither we call'd them all together, first Teedyuscung spoke to them by two Belts in behalf of the other Nations:

"Uncles, The Governor hath put these two Messengers into my Bosom & you have taken them out of my Bosom, I know nothing of your agreement with our Brn., you must answer for it. Then I spoke to them, first by a String.

"Brn. listen to what I am going to say, for I speak not for myself but in behalf of the great King, Onas, the Generals, Governors & all the Inhabitants on this Continant. Brn." When we first saw one another we always agreed as one Man & ever since have been as Brn. ought to be, when we met together we spoke plain from our Hearts before him who sees & knows the thoughts of all Men. Bror. I have heard you yesterday & I tell you I will go Home as you say, & make known to the King, Onas, the Generals & Governors, what you have said. Bror. you will remember that 2 Years ago, at the great Treaty in Easton, where 14 Nations were met, the great Road was cleared for all Messengers of Peace to Travel without hinderance or difficulty. Bror. you know that there came two Messengers from 14 Nations to the W.t.wd.[84] to our great Council Fire, they told us that they had clear'd the Road quite to Allegeny, & they requested it at the Council Fire, that I sho.d come to them, they had heard me Twice & they lik'd to hear and see me

---

[83] Joseph Croker, a workman helping Teedyuscung erect log cabins at Wyoming, was killed there by a Shawnee from Canisteo on May 27, 1758.

[84] I.e., westward.

once more. Bror. I let you know I am likewise Sorry In my Heart, for I have great Matters in Charge to deliver at the great Council. Bror. you know that it is the Custom for Messengers of Peace, not to open their Mouths till they come to the Place they are sent to. Bror. as you say that you are going to the Council, you will be pleas'd to let them know the reason why I must return back & cannot come to them. Bror., I let you know by this String, that it was agreed by our great Men, we sho.d go the great Kings Road;[85] it is entirely at the Indians own request that I came this Way to the Council & I hope you will not blame us that we are come hither.[86]

Gave 6 Strings

"Bror. you have heard already, that our great King hath been truly inform'd of all the Transactions between ye Indians & his Subjects, & that our King never intended to War against the Indians in any sort, he hath likewise given Orders to his Generals & Governors to settle every Thing to your Satisfaction,[87] & they have join'd their Hands in one to establish an Everlasting Peace with all the Indian Nations on a more firm foundation than ever Durable as the Mountains & to continue as long as Sun & Moon give Light.

"Bror. I'll let you know that not only my Heart is Sorry & painful, but the Hearts of our great Men will be fill'd with Sorrow & grief at try Return, for it never was heard of in any Nation that Messengers of Peace have been turn'd back without delivering their Message.

"Bror. I assure you from our great Men, that we realy pity your Youngmen Women & Children, & that is the reason we take so much Pains, Cost, & Labour to proclaim their Love & sincere Disposition towards all the Indian Nations, that so we may convince them that We seek nothing but their Welfare, & you will see & find that they who accept this Peace offer'd to them, will reap the Benefit, & they that do not care for it may blame themselves for the Consequence. Therefore Bretn. I desire you to have pity on your Young Men Women & Children, & perform your Promises &

---

[85] This is probably a reference to Braddock's Road to Fort Pitt, far to the south and running through territory secured by British forces a year earlier. Even if Post and company had the supplies to attempt such a journey, the time lost in the detour would certainly have caused them to miss the council.

[86] This statement is somewhat disingenuous, since Post was fully aware of the fact that Teedyuscung had been the one to bring the news of the Council to the Pennsylvania Government, and that he may not have been empowered to invite non-Indians to it.

[87] One can only wonder how Indian families ordered to return much-loved adopted captives against their will regarded such pronouncements.

Post Journal, June 17 continued

Engagements made at the Treaty in Easton, concerning our Flesh & Blood.

"Brn. Messengers of Peace pass free amongst all Nations, & sho.d they meet with 10,000 Warriors, they are not hurt by them. So I myself have treated with 800 Indians, besides French, at Fort Duquesne for 3 Days together & none hurt me. Brethrenl I would have you know, that I am not afraid either of Men or Devils, because I know I love him who is above us all, who hath all Power in Heaven & on Earth. I wish you all well.

Then Waponchako spoke to me as follows:

"Brother, we are pleased that you have granted our Request & have consented to return we realy think it is best so; for this Road has never been laid out, either by the Kings or Council, therefore it is not allow'd either for you or our Cousin to travel it, & it is moreover dangerous, I myself must go it blindfolded not being sure I shall not meet those who are grieved for the loss of Niagara, which makes it unsafe either for my Cousin or you to travel this Way. And we are indeed pleased that you have pity on the 5 Nations & the Delawares in returning home again, wishing you all a Safe Journey back. If you will still carry a Message to the Allegeny, you have the great Kings Road along which you may travel. When I return I will let you know what has been agreed on in the great council." They made us a Dinner & then we return'd back to our Lodgings.

Teedyuscung, for the Governors Information, spoke by a String as follows: "Brother! The Unamoas, Mohickons, Checohoky (or Nanticokes), Mennissings & Delawares, have all join'd in this good Peace, they have Strengthen'd it, by all putting their Hands to it as it has now been deliver'd by the English. Bror. you put these two Messengers into my Bosom, when I came as far as Passekachkung, the Mingoes there, took them out of my bosom & sent them back. As soon as they had taken them out of my Bosom, I consider'd that you & they have kept Council together these many Years. I do not know what you have agreed on, that you will know best.

"Brother! as your Message is with me I assure you it shall be known every where as far as I can come, I look upon it just as if your Messengers were with me still.

"Bror., altho' my Uncle has taken them out of my Bosom, yet I & my Warriors will see & keep our Eyes upon them that no Body may do them hurt."

We prepared for our Return. Quetaicond complained three Times to me, that he had Laboured very much to see the Prisoners deliver'd, & in this respect has had some loss, the 4 last Prisoners were brot. down by his Means. He had sent many Belts & Strings to the Government desiring a Horse & some Powder, because he is Old & cant' travel on Foot, that he might

Post Journal, June 17 continued

thereby be enabled to come down & speak with the Governor &c. To which he never rec'd any Answer. This discourageth him from speaking up for the English Interest. He told me, he had once brot. it so far, that all had consented to bring down their Prisoners but there was one yet that oppos'd it; many testify'd to me the Truth of this. He told me further; that Teedyuscung is in the fault that the Prisoners are not brot. down, because he hath taken upon himself the whole Rule & Management, excluding all others; Therefore they have left him alone to see how far he can bring it.

In consideration of this Mans Complaint, & seeing he was not able to Walk to Allegeny, I determin'd he sho.d have my spare Horse; which I made him a Present of in the Name of ye Governor & Inhabitants of Pensylvania, According to his former request to enable him to go on his journey; I also gave him a Stroud, a pr. Stockings & a pr. Spectacles, assuring him of your Love & Friendship. He was exceeding joyful, & Thank'd the Governor & all the People for their Love towards him; he said, now every Thing was fallen away from his Heart, Now his Heart was easy & good, & wish'd it might continue so all the Days of his Life.

The Message I had prepar'd in behalf of the Governmt. I this Day deliver'd to Teedyuscung, & is as follow's.

"Brethren at Allegeny! by this String I let you know it was agreed on at the Council Fire of all our great Men, that I sho.d accompany Teedyuscung to the great Councel at Allegeny, but when we came to Atsennetsing we rec.d a Message from the Mingoes, forbidding us to proceed any further, but to return back again, & threatning, That if I wo.d proceed they wo'd roast me; this Conduct towards me Surpris'd me much, being Charg'd with Matters of great Importance & Moment from the Government to you, which I am sure would be quite agreeable to you, & much to the benefit & satisfaction of yourselves, your Children & Grandchildren after you, & I hereby assure you, that my Heart remains in tender Love towards you, Praying to God our Father to bless & preserve you."

a String.

"Brethren at Allegeny! listen to what I have to say, you will remember when we first saw on another, we dug up & revived the Chain of Friendship which had been buried amongst you by the French, then the Dark Clouds were dispell'd & the Sun Shone over us & Warm'd us both. Brn. as soon as you heartily joyn'd in & agreed to the Peace concluded at Easton, the Storms ceased & the Day began to be bright & clear over us & all your Young Men

Post Journal, June 17 continued

Women & Children which co.d exercise their Understanding rejoic'd to see that Day. O may it continue whilst the Sun & Moon give Light. Now my Brn. at Allegeny, be Strong, you know that we have both joined our Hands together, & have Planted a Sprig in the Ground, I long to see how this Sprig grows, I wish it might become a mighty large Tree that its' Limbs may spread to the remotest Corners of the Earth, that all Nations may see it & be desirous to live & rest under the Shadow of this Tree of Peace.

"My Brn., let us stand & join together as One Man & finish that good & great Work we have begun.

A Bunch of Eight Strings

"Brethren, hearken to what I am going to say to you! I have the Pleasure to assure you, from Onas, the Governor, & all the Inhabitants of Pensylvania, of their Sincere Disposition to Peace, & that they will do their utmost not only to renew & Strengthen the former Friendship & Alliences, but to Settle all Things that may be likely hereafter to breed differences, to your entire Satisfaction, & likewise to observe & promote such a Friendly, Brotherly & affectionate Confidence, as will preserve a Mutual & lasting esteem & regard for each other. As a Proof of our Sincerity & Love towards you, I give you this Belt."

"Brethren, give Credit to what I say! I have it in Command to assure you from the General in & over all his Majesty's Forces on this whole Continent, that according to your request, made by me & Pisquitamen,[88] his Majesty has been truly Inform'd of all the Transactions between ye Indians & his Subjects; he was highly pleas'd to hear of your good Disposition for Peace, & I let you know, that he is a Tender Father to all his Children & Allies, hath given Orders to all his Generals & Governors, that there shall be, according to your request, a firm & Everlasting Peace between the Indians and all the Governments, on a more firm & lasting Foundation than ever, durable as the Mountains & as long as the Waters run, & Sun & Moon give Light." "Brethren, I let you know, that all our Generals & Governors will do their utmost to see this good Peace well establish'd."

"By this Belt I confirm all that has been deliver'd.

"And as a Seal of our Sincere Disposition, we give you this Belt of 15 Rows above a Yard long.

"Bror. Teedyuscung! When you arrive Safe at the great Council at Allegeny, you will be pleas'd to express high Satisfaction in finding the Road

---

[88] The brother of Tamaqua, the Delaware King, and an influential Delaware diplomat. See McConnell 1996 for an account of their closely entwined diplomatic careers. See also ff. 1, p. 26.

Tuesday, [June] 17th. We went up to the place where we had been often thretned if we Came they would Rost us, but they were Civel to us when there, altho one felow[38] Gave me a Great Blow across the Back as we were Going up to the town. Mr. Post Made a Speech, and their Answer was that they Desired us to pity their wemon and Children and Go Back, and we Must Go Back, then we Resolved we would not Insist any further, finding it was to no purpose, but Make ourselves Ready as soon as possible to Come home again.

[June] 17 Tustey we went over to the Please Where they Said they Would Rost us we went at 12 A clock and Staid there till 5 oures and had A confranenes with them and We Did Eat with them But they Said that we Must Go Back Then we Resolved that we Shold Go to Morow Morneng we sete Setled With one A Nother Old Tikcan[uu] is the chief of this Litel Town Pasecakung the 2 Tounes hase But one Name[w] the Mingo Chiefes Names we could Not find out But one Wapenga[ww] he Spock all He is the chife capten and I saw A Prisner Boy A Bout 9 or 10 yeares of Eadg they Say that there is 2 Neagors Lives in that Town That had Run from them inhabetenc and they Live in Packunk-cung there Wase one Pasikokung he was The Mane that killed Joseph Croker[xx]As we Went over to the Town he came Be hind Me and Strock me and Said that he Never would Love The White men any More and

---

[38]Identified in Hays's diary as a Shawnee man named Pasikokung.

[uu]Quitigon.

[w]The Delawares called it Passigachkunk, often shortened by the English to Secaughcung; the Mingoes knew it as Canisteo.

[ww]In his June 15 entry, Post identified this man as Wopenchachy (from the Delaware wapin tschachke, "a garfish'). His Iroquois name was Kinderunty, also translating as garfish, a prominent Seneca diplomat who played a major role in frontier negotiations throughout this period.

[xx]See ff. 82, p. 96.

Post Journal, June 17 continued

from thence to the Council Fire at Philadia. perfectly safe & easy to Travel in for them & their Children, & that they have nothing to fear.

"Brother, when they have laid hold on the Belt given them, & you find them well Dispos'd, then take this Belt on one End & give them the other & so lead them to our great Council Fire at Philadelphia. Bror. hollow very loud, If there should be any that think themselves Injur'd in Lands, or have any concerns in the Complaints made at the Treaty in Easton, or whatsoever else may lie heavy on their Minds, let them come & bring their Complaints, I assure them they shall readyly be heard & Justice done them. And for as much as this Matter is of Such great Consequence to them & their Posterity, So I desire you if possible to bring it about, that from all the Nation's there may come a certain Number of their Principle Men, as well Warriors as Members of Council, to Act for the whole Nation, & to bring a True & just Account of all the Transactions back again to their Nations, Bror. if they agree to come down, you will be pleas'd to give us timely Notice that we may provide for them in their Journey.

A Row Belt, A Man at each End,

above a Yard Long & 10 Rows.

"Brethren at Allegeny! I have finish'd what I had to say, however, one Thing I must bring closely to your remembrance, that is concerning our own Flesh & Blood amongst you, We have them very much at Heart & we wish to see them very soon amongst us; Pray grant our request & let us soon have the pleasure of seeing them

a Bunch of 8 Strings

Drove Along But My flesh creeped on My Back to think that I Must Bear Such usige of A Sevedges is Hand But I Laft and Said Nothing but Wish My Self out of thire Contry and he was a Shaner[y] One Rose in councel and Said that They were Poor Teveren keepers and Deare for he Got But 6 fulls of A Misher for a Ribond Stroud and it was so litel that hisKock[z] could Not Go in it and ~~he had But A litel one~~ Said he had But A Litel one kock Neither

[y] A Shawnee.
[z] A modest anatomical reference discreetly deleted from the journal.

[June] 19th. Early in the Morning we went to look for our Horses & made ready for our Return. The Persons appointed for our Escort were exceeding disagreeable to us, they we all from that Town which had threaten'd to Roast us, One of them was Jno Cook, French Margarets Son, who went from the Treaty of Easton to Murder at Allemengel, the other is Pashechqua, who kill'd Mr. Kroker at Waiomick,[89] the 3rd. had a Scalp hanging to his Breast & a Dutchman's Coat on, they ask'd us many Odd & out of the way Questions & seem'd to be Enemies to the English, we nevertheless behaved friendly to them, outwardly they appear'd likewise friendly, but we co.d discern falsehood in their discourse, & we realy thot. their whole Aim was to git us Secretly dispatch'd on the Way; abt. This Escort I inform'd Teedyuscung & declar'd my dislike, he seem'd concern'd & order'd one of his Young Men to go along with us. Moses Tattamy told Teedyuscung, he was afraid their whole affair would not turn out well; Teedyuscung answer'd him, that if he was afraid it wo.d be better for him to turn back again with us. We directly made ready & came off. At parting I wish'd Teedyuscung all the necessary Strength & Wisdom he stood in need of. We came to Billachkus,[90] who rec.d us very kindly; At the same Time there arriv'd a Messenger from Machachlosung[91] wanting to relieve a Prisoner.

[June] 20th. The Young Man & Tattamy scrupel'd going any further with us; We ask'd ye People in the Town, what they thot. if it was advisable for us to go in this Company, they all to a Man advis'd us to the contrary, desiring us to stay till the Messenger went back to Machkachlosung, when we might be Convoy'd by them. So I told the Mingoes & Shawanos who accompany'd us hither, that I co.d not go with them having some business to do with the People in this Place. Some bad Men amongst them, instigated by the Wicked-one, have rais'd Lying Stories, telling ye People that no body knew rightly my Message, they also said, that they had heard I sho.d have told Ashkunachkung in Atsennetsing, that I had order to take good Notice of their Land, Rivers, Towns & Strength, for that after my return they sho.d git no more Powder or any Thing else, for it was intended by the English to drive them all out & possess themselves of their Land; they likewise said that Moses Tattamy had said something to ye same purpose.

---

[89] The same Shawnee man who struck John Hays across the back a few days earlier. See p. 101.

[90] John Hays's journal records they visited with James Davis this day. Billachkus is probably one of his Indian names.

[91] Wyalusing. See ff. 22, p. 46.

Wednesday, [June] 18th. Waited all Day for an Escort to Conduct us safe Back again; Quitigon Made a Great Complaint that he had don a great Deal for the English, but had never Got any Reward for it, and that he had no horse, so we Concluded to Give him, in the Name of the Governour, the horse and Sadle that I Rode to Go to Alegeny Very Wet Wether.

[June] 18 Wensdy we left he king We waited All Day for a Pilet to conduct us Back Agen It wase Wete in they Morning But it cleared up and then we Give the Soral hors to king Tikeun and Sedel and Bridel and fited him for the Jorney to Alganey We Expect to Go Moro Early of

Thursday, [June] 19th. Took Leave of our felow travilers and Set of home, altho we were not Sory to Leave that place, yet we were Sory to turn Back so fruitless. The King Sent Moses, and the Mohawks sent four of their young men with us as far as James Davises, where we Stayed all night.

[June] 19 Thurdy We heared Sum Ling Stories we Set of from compeny Packung Without A teare and it wase ~~Body~~ A Bout Ten A cloace We had in compeney 4 Mohakes and Moseas Tatemy the 4 John Koock[aaa] And the Shayner That killed Joseph croker For A Bout 6 Miles the inding are Seteled All A Long the River then Cushinsten Town Where the Moncy chief Lives[bbb] and there Lives No More Till we com to James Davis

Friday, [June] 20th. Waited for an Escort and were Very Kindly used; this is an Ordinary Country, Nothing but Mountains and Rocks, and pine timber, save the small Low lands the Indians plants their Corn on.

[June] 20 Fridey we were A Bleadged to Weite for A Scort that day it Rained and Wase Very wat the Were Vert kind to us the Neame of that Pleace is O̶ Wopackung. . [ccc] Very

---

[aaa] John Cook, French Margaret's grandson.
[Bbb] See ff. 57, p. 82. Also known as Hog Town.
[ccc] See ff. 56, p. 80.

[June] 21st. The people from Atsennetsing arriv'd here, I call'd them all together & spoke to Ashkunachang by a String. "I have heard a Tale here which I now inform you of, & I desire you to speak the Truth before all these People if I have said any such Thing, if not then I require you & all here Present to tell them that speak such Lying Stories that the Devil is their Master & hath infus'd such lies into their Hearts in Order to raise Sedition & Disturbances. For such Words never enter'd my Thoughts, much less came out of my Mouth."

Achkunachang then declared before all the People that I never had said any such Thing to him.

Now Brn. said I, I must tell you by this oportunity, that Envy, Suspicion & Lies, are such bad Things, wherewith The Wicked-One poisoneth your Minds, nor can you ever live in Peace & Quietness untill you turn to God & let him take those bad Things out of your Hearts &c. Moses Scrupel'd to go any further with us, I told him he sho.d consider well of it, for his turning back again might prove of bad Consequence. He said: the People in Philadia. had told him before, that I was of such a Disposition that I always wo.d have my own Way, & that therefore he did not care to be directed by me.

[June] 22nd. I ask'd Moses Tattamy if he had any Thing to say? He reply'd that he co.d not see any reason for his returning to Philadia., that the Friends trusted no body but him, & reposed their whole Confidence in him, if he sho.d return they wo.d blame him for ever, seeing they expected to know the Truth by him. I am resolv'd therefore to proceed forward. So we parted. We came that Day 3 Miles to the other Side where French Margaret lives, & were exceeding glad to have trusty Men for our Companions instead of those Murderers.

timbery Sort of Low Land from that to Cuskise[ddd] and very Taul Pines But it is Not Good For anything and The hiles is good for Nothing They are All Swampes and Piness the King Said that He Would Go of this Day in his Jorney For Alegeney we Pearted With them yesterdy the 19 of June

Saturday [June] 21st   Very Rainy Wether; waited still for an Escort.

[June] 21 Seterdy I saw a Prisneres that Wase taken in Virgeney his Name Wase Wagner his Father was Killed he Lives in the Mingo contry I saw A Girel of 3 or 4 years old that Man Spoak to me he was A Bout 22 Years of eadg

Sunday, [June] 22d. Moses Tatemy, altho' Ordered to Come home with us, Left us this Day, saying he had some Business to Do for the Quakers, and could not Know what to say to the Quakers if he Did not Go along, and would not Come any further with us, but went after Teedyuscung, we Got an Escort and Set of and traveled smartly till we came to Asinsan, and had some Discourse with Egho-howin,[41] the Governour of the town who told us he had no orders from the Mingoes to Bring in any prisnors, and he Did not Mind Teedyuscung, seeing he had no orders from them, pased on Untill Night and Lodged in the Woods.

[June] 22 Sundy this Morning we Pearted With Moses Tatemy he went Back A Gean to the King and We have Got A Scort to Go with us We came to a Cree[k] [eee] and it was so hie That I was Ableadged to take my Bage on my Shold er and Go throw to Asoinsen[fff] and Daves[ggg] Left us and We came on till Night Picht our camp one the River Side there are Very fine Low Lands and tall Pines Timber

---

[ddd] See ff. 57, p. 82.
[eee] Probably Cochocton River.
[fff] Assinisink.
[ggg] James Davis.

---

[39] See ff. 46, p. 72

[June] 23rd. We Breakfasted at French Margarets. She told us that she had heard, her Character was quite spoil'd among the White Inhabitants, who charged her with having burned one of the White Prisoners, which she said was not true. The Woman said to be burn'd is here, you can ask her yourself what I have done to her? I have also heard, said She, Mr. Peters[92] has given Orders, that if I am catch'd I shall be put in Prison. That the storekeeper at Shomoko had told her she wo.d git nothing for ye 4 Prisoners she had with her, altho' she had bot. them with her own Money, & her Daughter had given £7- with 5 Strouds, 7 Shirts, & 3 pr. Stockings for one. & Therefore desires to know if this will be paid to her. She says she is afraid to come amongst the Inhabitants because of these threatnings, also she wo.d gladly bring the Prisoners down. It Raind very hard this whole Day, we were very wet but came nevertheless to Diaogo.

[June] 24th. In hunting our Horses amongst the high Woods we were as wet as if we had Waded thro' a River. The Diaogo was very high, we work'd very hard above half the Day & in Danger of our Lives, before we co.d git over with our Horses because the Canoe was so Small. We came to Machacklosung, it rain'd the whole Day, & the Water rose so high that it was impossible to git over. The whole Night we were so plagued with Musquittos & Gnats, that it was impossible for us to close our eyes.

---

[92] Richard Peters, then Pennsylvania Provincial Secretary.

Mond'y [June] 23d. It Rained very hard but we Set off and Came to French Margrets[40] about ten o'Clock and Got Breakfast; She being very Kind she made Complaint and said she Did not Know what to do, for she had been ill used at Shomokin,[41] and threatned, and that they told her that Mr. Petters[42] had Said That hir and hir family should be apprehended, and She said she had some prisnors She wanted to Bring Down, but Durst not Bring them, But we promised hir protection and Safety if She Came the Road, by fort Allen, Notwith standing it Rained, we Set of and came to Diahoga and stayed there all Night.

Tuesday, [June] 24th. The River was Very high and Dificult to Cross but we Swam our Horses over and Got a Canoe for our selves and Baggage, and pushed on over hills and Mountains, an Extream bad Road; and Cam to Quihaloosing Creek after Dark, but could not Get Over in to the town, so we made fires and stayd all Night.

[June] 23 Mundy It Rained very hard we came ~~th~~ to frensh Marget A bout 10 A clock and She was very cind and Spoak very faire and Said that She Did Not know what to Dow for She was ill used at Shomoking and Thretned and that Peters Said they Should be a APrehended and that Caty[hhh] had Promesed to Deliver the Prisners and I Promest her Prottion to Town we came to ~~Toigo~~ Tiogo and Lodg there that Nigt

[June] 24 Tusdy Digoa River and Siskhaney Two miles up is Not 20 Rods A Pert Dioag was very high we Sweamed Our horses over with Much Defickelty and Set of for Mochilucan But the Mountens was so Bade that we could Not Get along we crosed 2 Montanes Mountenys and when we came to the Creek we cold Not Go over that Night we in camped But the Neates wase Lik to Eate us up With Deficktely we Got over To the Town Where we Got Whete cakes and A very good

---

[40] A niece of the well-known frontier diplomat Madame Montour, French Margaret and her people were living near present-day Elmira, New York in 1760.

[41] She had visited Fort Augusta at Shamokin to trade a month earlier.

[42] Although she refers to Pennsylvania Provincial Secretary Richard Peters as the source of the threat, its actual origin probably may be traced to post commander Hugh Mercer or the local provincial agent, Nathaniel Holland.

[hhh] Margaret's daughter Catherine.

[June] 25th. With Difficulty we came safe over the Water, the People here received us kindly & desired us to rest ourselves there that Day, which we accepted of & dry'd our Wet Cloaths. Here we saw an odd sort of Heathenish Dance, which I never met with before. They appointed a Guide to go with us.

[June] 26th. about 9 oClock we set off. John Rogers went with us, it Rain'd very hard the whole Day & the Path was exceeding bad to find & travel. At the Susquehannah we providentially found a Canoe, which was of great Service to us, we took it along above 60 Miles, quite down to Waiomick. It was very wet & Slippery & very hard for our poor Horses to climb up those Mountains & great Rocks, both we & they had many a fall, we often thought our Horses would be kill'd. In Tinkkaneck we were much afraid our Horses would have been drown'd, because of the Steepness of the Bank of the Creek, being oblig'd to Swim so far about before any place could be found for them to come out of the Water. The Airs was full & the Ground cover'd with Gnats, they plagued & tormented us much, they are worse than an Enemy to fight with, they mind neither Fire Smoak, nor Rain, our Skin's burn'd as if we had been whip'd with Nettles, We long'd much for Day to be deliver'd out of this Purgatory.

Wednesday, [June] 25th. Got over in the Morning to Quickaloosing with Dificulty, and Stayed all Day waiting for an Escort and Guide.

[June] 25 ~~W~~ Wensdy Breackfast and they Went in councel

Tobe Deanes came in compeny With us till here and Another Man and we Lay here this Day and Liveis Well the had A Sort of Worship and they Dansed Round and Two Beat the Skine and Wemen and Men A Religes Dance

Thursday, [June] 26th. Set off and John Rodgers[43] Came with us, it Began to Rain very hard, we Got a canoo & Rodgers went in it, and took our Bagage by watter, and we Rode along Shore we met about noon and Eat something, then I took the Canoo my spell till night, and swamed our Horses over a great Creek and Stayd there all Night, but little sleep, the Knates Bit so hard.

[June] 26 Thurdy we Set of and John Rodger To A Scort us to Wimeang and it did Rain Very hard and we Got A canow and John Went in the can-now and Took our Luges and Mr Post and I Went Singel horce Then we Met A Gen and I Went in the cannow My torn till Night and we came to A Learg creeak[iii] and wase A Bleadged to Sweam The horces over it and there we camped it Rained very hard and the Nates Wase So Plenty that We could harly Live for them I got No Sleepe in the Mrning ~~F~~ horses was Blue With them it Rained on All Night

---

[43] An Indian residing at Wyalusing.

[iii] Identified as Tinkkaneck, Tunkhannock Creek., in Post's entry for the day.

[June] 27th. Not being able to sleep, we thank'd God for ye Day Light & made haste away. It Rain'd hard all Day, the River was high & our Horses oblidg'd to Swim many Times. When we came to Lechchowichlao we let our Horses feed a little before we Swam them thro', here the poor Creatures had enough to do to git over, when they had almost got up the Bank they would often fall back again into the Water. The difficulties to be encounter'd on such Journeys are hardly to be described. However we arrived safe at Waiomick & thank'd the Lord who had brot. us so far Safe.

[June] 28th. Our Cloaths & all our Things were wet, it was a foggy Morning, nevertheless we set out abt. 10 oClock, had many Gusts Rain, & came in the Evening to Moshwatschowal, It Raind hard the whole Night.

Friday, [June] 27th. Very Rainy weather Mr. Post took the Canoo this Morning and the Horses, and about Eleven o'Clock we came to a narow pass wher the horses, with Hight of the River, was oblidged to Swime a considerable way, and had to all in the Canoo, then took our horses again and had to Swim another Large Creek & Climbe many a hill, so that our horses were almost wore out, but at Lenth we Got to Weoming, thank God.

[June] 27 Fridey Set of very early it Rained Still M Mr Post Took the cannow and we met him at A hill Where the hill and the River Met in A Streat Pashedg where the horces had to Sweam we had to go in the cannow A Great Pease then we Set of agen Then we came to A Nother creeak[iii] and wase A Bleadged to Sweam the horces A Gene and The hiles was Very Slipey the horces Got Maney A Dispert Falle we thought theire Bones wold be Broken uvery Minet it Sleacked Raining With Defickelty we came to Wioming that Night and wase Thankfull for our Safe A Rvel there But I Saw A Sthreangthing thing that Sum Inding Had Doon he had Maid Sume Trackes in A hard hill with His feete and Struck A whit Oack tree Strokes With his fist till he Had Nocked of the Bark and Broke the Wood With his fist- NotBney[kkk] I Saw 3 Prisneres at Frensh Margetes Dwelling That was the Last I saw

Saturday [June] 28 Set of from Weoming and traveled Over the Mountains and Lodged in the woods and had Very wet Weather

[June] 28 Seterdy it is A Hease Morning We Set of and Soforth
   By Mee John Hays

[iii]Identified as Lechchowichlao, Lackawanna River, in Post's entry of the day.
[kkk] Nota Bene.

[June] 29th. In climbing so many Hills & Mountains in our Way, this Day spent & weaken'd us much. The Lehi was very high, but by Gods help we sat our Horses & Swam safe thro', and in the Evening arriv'd at Fort Allen &c.

[June] 30th. At Bethlehem.

Now I thank my God & Saviour who has had his Eye upon us, Carried us upon his Wings & so graciously brought us thro' all Dangers, by Day & Night. Tho' the Proud Heathen have laid many Snares, & often open'd their Mouths to devour us yet Notwithstanding our gracious God & Saviour hath help'd us thro' & deliver'd us from their Subtilty & Wickedness & brought us again safely & happily into the Land of the Living, for which I thank him with Joy & Gladness.

Sunday, [June] 29th. Set out Early and
it Rained, we Rod Lehi so Deep that ye
water Came over the Horses withers,
and Arived at fort Allen at five o'Clock.

Monday, [June] 30th. Set of Early and
came to my fathers against Noon &c
&c

The following ledger entries appear farther on in the manuscript:

A. Jo John Hays did Enter in the Servics With Fredrick Post and caption Bull May
the 5- 1760
B. May the 16   1760
  I ame in Deat to Mis Poist
  For Mockison Leather   L S P
        John Hays   0 2 6
June the 16th   2
To A Hundred Wampum
I Got from Mr Mr Post
and half A hundred wampem
For the colection
To /June the 18-1760
The King Had a Shirt of Mee at   L S P
By Isaac Still Deat Balens
and it Comes to.........1-8-6
the 17 To a Shirt   0 18 0
& to A pere of Mockeson 0 5 0
        Totell   2:6.6
June   the 3   1760
Moses Teatemy is in Deat
for A Peare of Stokens 00 5 and 6

ASSOCIATED DOCUMENTS:

AFTERMATH

TIMOTHY HORSFIELD TO R. PETERS, 1760.[1]

Sir,

I have desired tbe bearer, Fri^d Rote, to ride before and inform you of this Troublesome visit of ye Indian man Pofoonham & Companions, 25 in number; they have three White children Captives, and some Horses stolen from the Frontiers, which they are desirous to deliver to his Honour. I have ordered Rote to take the Tavern Keepers Bills of Exchange from place to place, to be given the Gentlemen Commissioners. Please to Excuse hast, from S^r,

Your most H'ble Serv't,

TIM. HORSFIELD.

Beth'm, July 8, 1760.

Directed.
To Richard Peters, Esquire, Philada.

FREDERICK POST'S RELATION OF WHAT PASSED BETWEEN HIM AND THE QUAKER, OR RELIGIOUS INDIANS, AT MONMUCHLOOSON [WYALUSING], ON THE SUSQUEHANNAH[2]

Original Transcript	*Transliteration*
Br., last fall wan you past bay hear, I hoard wot you and your Brodarn da Englysch had agread on, I rasayst over it to hoar you, affter you com back, dat was the ryson I dalywered you da hosses dat was brot haer from de inhabetans back; Br. Listen wat I say, I have hart	Brother, last fall when you passed by here, I heard what you and your brethren the English had agreed on, I rejoiced over it to hear you, after you come back, that was the reason I delivered you the horses that was brought from the inhabitants back; Brother listen what I say, I have heard

---

[1] Published in Hazard 91852b [3]: 741-42.)

[2] Published in Hazard (1852b[3]:742-44). See p. 122 below for a reference to this document in the Minutes of the Provincial Council.

you last nayt, you told me wat our brodern de Englysch have so mouts at heart, and wat the da sayr, we all lat you know it schall be grantet what da dosayr consarnying dar one flasch and blod, we know dat Got has sean us; we still have kapt your flasch and blod hear; we know dat Gott Nous us we have not bean onnest; we have bean falsch and hepocreasey in keeping you flasch and blod so long back, for all we tat to love Gott br, but nowa we all tall and aschur you, all dat belongs to Deas taun or Susayetey, we got displeast har which we will dalever to you, for we dasayr to do Schoustus and love Gott, br, but we connot command odears nouley com her to dalever dam allso; br, now I woult frilay do wat our br'n da Englysh dasayrd me to do, I wist it was in may pour to asseast, dat da may got all dam back dat ar Scadert in sa wouds, every war geave a string a string of wompom. Da boys nam is Schacob, from Tulpekkay, Da woman is born in bat Fort in Nuangland, har nam is Mary, da garlls nam is Janckke, Alodats garl, har parns leave at Memesing, her faders nam is Peter Sonnet; da Schyldern crayd as if da schould day wan de war prasantat to us; Deas poepel has bout dam from oders.

Dear and honoured Sir, it gywess my grat pleasur to inform your honnnour in may myecknes, of halt dat we arayst at Mockocklocking, an Inschan taun nuly layd out, war dar ar a Companie to gader all of da Manyssing Indeans, a sord of raleceous poepel, it is

you last night, you told me what our brethren the English have so much at heart, and what they desire, we all let you know it shall be granted what they desire concerning their one flesh and blood, we know that God has seen us; we still have kept your flesh and blood here; we know that God knows us we have not been honest; we have been false and hypocrites in keeping your flesh and blood so long back, for all we try to love God brother, but now we all tell and assure you, all that belongs to this town or society, we got displaced here which we will deliver to you, for we desire to do justice and love God, brother, but we cannot command others newly come here to deliver them also; brother, now I would freely do what our brethren the English desired me to do, I wished it was in my power to assist, that they may all them back that are scattered in the woods, everywhere[.] Give a string of Wampum. The boys name is Jacob, from Tulpekkay, the woman is born in that Fort in New England, her name is Mary, the girls name is Jancke, a Low Dutch girl, her parents live at Memesing, her father's name is Peter Sonnet; the children cried as if they should die when they were presented to us; These people has bought them from others.

Dear and honored Sir, it gives me great pleasure to inform your honor in my meekness, of all that we arranged at Mockocklocking, an Indian town newly laid out, where there are a company together, all of the Manyssing Indians, a sort of religious people, it is about 8

about 8 Yoahr wan da bagon an Papounnahang, is da bageanner of da compane, and dar menester da want to sea da frinds scheaflay, and to stho dat da raly ar frynds, da have not schagnd in da warr dam prisnors da have; dam poepel ar synds com to leave amongst dam, and da ar datarmd to lat nobode leave amongst dam dat do not daleaver dar proasonars an Indeans dat have not schaynd in da wahr, do not layck to tryt about peass, so dar of da sam sort so far as I coan larn, is all in querralnas; da wat for ous, but I sea mor and mor of a letel dastorbans amongst dam, and da apt to beleave it will bryd a war battwen dam and da Mohocks; as deas poepel is a ralegeous poepel, and da dasyrd of me to hold meting to dam, so I deat with grat bleasing over da tackts, dat da anschals proclaymd bay boyrd of aur Saveyur Jesus Christ, it sutel wall da deat daleaver da prosoners to us, as it is in Tetyuskunds latear bay dais Speaces as follows:

Br'n, geave yut attanceon to wat I say, affter we want to counsel bay aursalfss, I told Titeyoscond mane ting war on he had not tod bafor, he sad, Br., I on I have not don as I schould; I schould had mor confard with you on da rod, dan we mat ogan war; we tanckt dam, of Onas da Governor and all da inhabetans, of dar sensear deasposeschan toward peas, an I gave dam a string of wompom. Sir, I bag hartly to be excust, not rayting a very cearcumstans, am may speceas to dam in da fyrs part. I am Schicks, so dat I schust can ster and dat is all, an I am aschamed to rayt,

years when they began and Papounnahang is the beginner of the company and their minister, they want to see their friends safely, and to show that they really are friends, they have not joined in the war. Them prisoners they have; Them people are since come to live amongst them, and they are determined to let nobody live amongst them that do not deliver their prisoners and Indians that have not joined in the war, do not like to treat about peace, so there are of the same sort so far as I can learn, is all in earnest; They wait for us, but I see more and more of a little disturbance amongst them, and they apt to believe it will breed a war between them and the Mohocks; as these people is a religious people, and they desired of me to hold a meeting to them, so I did with great blessing over the tracts, that the angels proclaimed by birth of our savior Jesus Christ, it subtle will that did deliver the prisoners to us, as it is in Tetyuskund's later by these speeches as follows:

Brethren, give your attention to what I go to say, after we went to council by ourselves, I told Titeyoscond many things where on he had not told before, he said, Brother, I on I have not done as I should; I should had more conferred with you on the road, then we met again where; we thanked them, of Onas the Governor and all the inhabitants, of their sincere disposition toward peace, and I gave them a string of Wampum. Sir, I beg heartily to be excused, not writing a very circumstance, and make speeches to them in the first part. I am sick, so that I just can stir and that is all, and I am ashamed to write, bad as I write in free hand in the field, without table or chair, and the mosquitoes and sand fleas takes all courage most away, it has many more unconveniences besets this man's hand, in the evening they delivered another string, with these words: Brother, I am greatly pleased to hear of that good peace, that it is well established I heartily share in it, and like to live in peace, hearken Brother I pray you would have some pity on us, and let us have no strong liquor at all, this we all beg of you that live at the place called Machachlosung, and if any of our young man should come down, ask them where they came from, and when they say they come from Machachlosung, I pray you give them not a drop of liquor at all, and I hope you will hear us. Give a string, as hitherto we have come over along. Our company consists of 14 in number. I beg heartily to be excused in writing any more, and I beg to be remembered by all the gentle people sirs. I remain your most humble and obedient servant.

FREDERICK POST.

The reason why I break off from writing so soon, our hosts arrived, and they call us once more together to have a meeting.

I remain with respect, your honest

Humble and obedient servant,

To his honor the Governor of Pennsylvania:

Brother, I came to Machochlaung,

mane Indeans lyve, I cald dam all togader, and I told dam wat we bous had agread on wan we sa one anoder last, and wat you ar sorre for and have so mouts at hart, and dassyrt me to mack it avere war noun avere war, and dasayrd dam to be strong and sea dat your flasch and blod may be rastord to you; now br'r, you know dat it is aur agreamand, dat as soun as I hoar any ting, I geave yu daracktly notys of, and as I am as jat closs bay you, so I sand prasonars to you which da daleverat to me, and I geave dam to Papunnahanck to dalever dam to you; br. I do not sand deas poepel daun, da have had damsalf a long dasayr to go daun to sea dar br. da Englesch, so I tot it proper to sand dam along; I hop you will rajoys to sea dam and be kaynd to dam, and allso to dam poepel dat bryng dam daun; wan I am farder from you and I schall meat wit som, I schall bryng dam maysalf daun wan I com along; br. you know aur worck is grat, and will tack a long taym befor we coan com bacvk, I salud all da schandel pepel, and dasayr you to be strong.

Ye 20 Day of May, 1760, rot at Machochloschung.

where many Indians live, I called them all together, and I told them what we both had agreed on when we saw one another last, and what you are sorry for and have so much at heart, and desired me to make it everywhere known everywhere, and desired them to be strong and see that your flesh and blood may be restored to you; now brother, you know that is our agreement, that as soon as I hear anything, I give you directly notice of, and as I am as yet close by you, so I send these prisoners to you which they delivered to me, and I give them to Papunnahanck to deliver them to you; brother I do not send these people down, they have had themselves a long desire ro go down to see their brethren the English, so that I thought it proper to send them along; I hope you will rejoice to see them and be kind to them, and also to them people that bring them down; when I am farther from you and I shall meet with some, I shall bring them myself down when I come along; brother you know our work is great, and will take a long time before we can come back, I salute all the gentle people, and, desire you to be strong.

The 20 Day of May, 1760, Written at Machochloschung.

PENNSYLVANIA PROVINCIAL COUNCIL MINUTES[3]
AT A COUNCIL HELD AT THE STATE HOUSE,
FRIDAY THE 11ᵀᴴ JULY, 1760.

Present:
The Honourable JAMES HAMILTON, Esqr., Lieutenant Governor.

Benjamin Shoemaker,	Joseph Turner,	
Richard Peters,	Thos. Cadwallader,	Esquires
Mr. Fox,		Gentlemen of
Mr. Pemberton,		the City
Frederick Post, Interpreter.		

24 Minisink Indians, 2 Nanticokes, and 3 Delawares, from an Indian Town called Michalloasen, or Wighaloosan, about Fifty or Sixty Miles above Wiomink, on the susquehannah, vizt.:

Papoununk,	
Toan-kakanan,	Two Speakers of the Minisink Indians; with
Noosawapamukus,	
Machine-uka,	Nanticokes at Chenango,
Nanatchies, Delaware.	
Pelawe-ach, Minisink.	
Sepeank, Minisink.	
Tatankaing, Minisink.	
Mesakeenan, Minisink.	
Penacheewees, Minisink.	
Kendaskond,	
Wesehannas,	Minisinks from Atsintsink.
Onape-assen, Minisink.	
Job Chillaway, Delaware.	
Wayajoe-quas.	
Three Women and Nine Children.	

---

[3] Published in Hazard (1852a [8]:484-500).

Papunhack arose and spoke as follows, Job Chillaway, a Delaware Indian, being Interpreter:

"Brother:

"Hearken to me; Teedyuscung called at our town in his way to Atsintzing, and we held a Council together, in which he related to us all the business he was then going about, and likewise applied to us to assist him in the matter, which he said you had very much at heart, vizt.: The return of your flesh and Blood that were prisoners amongst us; We were very well pleased with the good News he brought, and with his request, it made our hearts glad, and we did as he desired, giving him up in Council the three only Prisoners we had amongst us."

A String.

"Brother:

"We told Teedyuscung we intended to go to Philadelphia soon, and thereupon he desired us to take the Three English Captives that we had delivered to him in Council, down with us, and deliver them to the Governor. And Frederick Post wrote down, as well what Teedyuscung said to us, as what We said to him, and give us the Writing which I now deliver to you, as it contains all that passed between us."

Here he delivered the writing and the Prisoners to the Governor.

N.B. The writings were read, and are the same with what are inserted in Frederick Post's Journal.

One of them was a Girl of the name of Vanellen, and was given to her Brother, who came on purpose to receive her, a Letter having been sent to him from Bethlehem, to acquaint him that she was come with these Indians. The other two being a Boy and Girl, were committed to the care of Mr. Fox, and he promised to provide for them and send them to their relations.

He then proceeded in his speech, saying:

"Brother:

"After Teedyuscung was gone, We consulted among ourselves, and determined to seek for and collect all the Horses that had been stolen from the Frontiers of your Province, and brought to our parts; We found Six and took them along with us; One was drowned in Crossing the Sasquehannah at Wioming; Another was claimed on the road, and Job Chillaway went back with the horse to the Moravian Tavern, along with the Dutchman that claimed it, and desired Justice Horsefield that he might be examined, and if it was proved to be his property, that he might have it. Another being a young Coult, tired on the road, and was left at a Smith's Shop, about two Miles on this Side Samuel Deans; Three we have brought with us, and they are here in Town.

"Brother, I have done."

Then Toan-kakanan arose, and also spoke:

"Brother:

"Tho' we are poor, we want no recompence for the prisoners and Horses; We do not return them to you from a desire of gain; you are welcome to them, and we are glad of this opportunity of obliging you.

"Brother:

"I am now to acquaint you that We have a White Man in our Town, who Chose to live amongst us. We know not where he comes From; He is a good man, and we are glad to keep him among us. One of the Nanticoke Indians said he was a soldier, and left the soldiers at Some place on the Mowhawks River; He was tired with soldiering, and chose to come and live with the Indians; He was at Chenango before he Came to us. His name is [   ] Fazier, and he desires the Governor will give him his discharge."

Then the Minisink Chief proceeded: "Brother: several English Men have come to our Town, but in a little while they did not behave well, and We did not like them; But this Man has always behaved well. We desire the Governor would send him his discharge by us, that he may either stay or come as he pleases, for we leave him entirely at his liberty. He is beloved by us all.

"Brother:

"I assure you We have no more Prisoners nor Horses in our Town. We have cleared ourselves of them all, but I think it proper to acquaint you that one of our old Men, called Allemarvein, tho' blind, assisted us very much in the Matter of the Horses, he bought some of them from those who had taken them from the English, and tho' they Cost him Money, yet he did not Value it, he gave them to us Chearfully, and desired We Would take them safe to you; We are not like many other Indians, who will neither deliver their prisoners or their Horses, nor let those do it who are otherwise well disposed.

"This is all We have to say."

The Governor returned them thanks for their speeches; told them he would send a Letter by them to the soldier, in whose favour they had spoken, and desired they would attend to-Morrow Morning at Nine O'Clock, when he would say something to them.

At a Council held in the Stadt House, on Saturday the 12ᵀᴴ July, 1760.

Present:

The Honourable JAMES HAMILTON, Esqr., Lieutenant Governor.

Benjamin Shoemaker,	Richard Peters, Esqrs,
Joseph Fox,	Jeremiah Warder,
John Reynold,	Joseph Morris,
Hugh Roberts,	Richard Wister,
Owen Jones,	Thomas Say,
Israel Pemberton,	Several and others of the Society call'd Quakers.

The same Indians as yesterday.

The Governor desired the Interpreters to acquaint the Indians that he was going to give them his Answer to their speeches, & then began as follows, vizt.:

"Brothers:

"What you said yesterday was very pleasing, and, in behalf of Myself, and all the Inhabitants of this Province, I thank you for Complying with our request, which We have so much at heart, and for the pains and labour you have been at in coming to us, and restoring our flesh and Blood to us."

A string.

"Brothers:

"We all rejoice to see the upright and Good part you have acted. We desire you will be strong and use your utmost endeavors to prevail on all other Indians to follow your Example and do the same good thing, and for your encouragement We present you with this Belt."

A Belt.

"Brothers:

"We are very sensible as well as you of the mischiefs that are ever arising from an intemperate use of strong Liquors, but it is not in our power to restrain our people that are at so great distance from this City, from Carrying Rum to your Towns. There is no other way to put a Effectual stop to this, but for you to stave every Cask that is brought among you. Be strong and let no one escape, and these bad men will be discouraged from bringing you any more Rum."

A String.

"Brothers:

"As a token of our Love for you, We have provided a few things for you, and desire your acceptance of them.

"Brothers:

"We have been told that there are some of our Prisoners with French Margaret, and that she would come and deliver them up to us, but has heard some stories which make her afraid to come. Pray give her this string, and let her know that she may come to us without any danger, and that we shall be glad to see her with all the prisoners as soon as possible."

A string.

"Brothers:

"In Complyance with your request, I have wrote a Letter to the young man, and have promised him my protection, so that he may come down with safety, and as soon as he pleases.

"I have now done."

The Indians, who were very attentive, after a little Consultation returned the Governor their hearty thanks, and after a Considerable pause Papoonhack, seemingly under a good deal of concern, arose and spoke as follows:

"Brothers:

"I do not come here to do any public Business with the Government. I am not in that Character. I came on a religious account, on an Invitation sent me by some Religious People, about twelve Months ago, and therefore it frightens me to hear what you just now spoke, vizt: that you have provided some Goods for our use, and mean to make us a Present of them. I thank you for your good will, but I cannot allow myself to receive them, since this would look as if I was come as other great ones do to receive presents. No, Brother, I am perfectly satisfied with the many Good things I have heard in the Religious Conferences that We have held since we came here.

"Brother:

"I will tell you the Reason why I say I am frighten'd; should I lay my hands on your presents, it would raise a Jealousy in the Breasts of those round about me, who transact the publick Business and are wont to receive Presents on such Occasions. It would, moreover, be apt to corrupt my own mind, and make me proud, and others would think I wanted to be a great Man, which is not the case. I think on God, who made us, and want to be instructed in his service and Worship. I am a great Lover of Peace. I have never been concern'd in War Affairs. I have a sincere remembrance of the old Friendship which subsisted between the Indians and your forefathers, and shall always observe it. I love my Brethren, the English, and they shall ever find me faithful. I was invited to come, and for these reasons did come, and not to receive Presents, which spoil and corrupt the receivers of them.

Many have misbehaved after they have received them, and many, I am afraid, came only for the sake of Receiving them.

"Brother:

"It comes into my mind to mention something to you that I Think wrong in your dealings with the Indians. You make it publick that you will give a Certain price for our Skins, and that they are to be weighed and paid for at that set price, according to their Weight. Brother, there are two bad things done in this way of dealing; You alter the price that you say you will give for our skins, which can never be right; God can not be pleased to see the prices of one and the same thing so often altered and changed; our Young Men, finding that they are to receive for their skins according to the weight, play tricks with them and leave on them several parts which are of no use, only to make them weigh more, such as some of the flesh, the Ears, and the paws.

"Brother:

"This is not as it ought to be; we should not skin our skins in such a way; our Corrupt heart has found out this way of dealing. Brother, you see there is no Love nor honesty on either side. You do wrong in altering your prices, and the Indians do wrong in bringing skins with so much badness on them. Therefore, Brother, we propose to fling this entirely away, for if it remains so we shall never agree and love one another as Brothers do. Now Brother, I desire you will not raise your Goods to too high price, but lower them so as you can afford it, that we may live and walk together in one Brotherly Love and Friendship, as Brothers ought to live. Brother, I don't say this with a view to have a great Price for my skins, but only lay it before you that you may Consider and Come to some determination about it.

"Brother:

"I must once more acquaint you That my Chief design in Making this Visit is to confer about Religious Matters, and that our Young Men agree with me in this, and to love God, and to leave off their former bad courses."

He then produced an old Bill of the New Jersey Currency, that is out of date, and Complained that it was given him for skins, and nobody would take it in payment. The Governor gave him present Currency for it, with which he was satisfied.

Job Chillaway made a Complaint on behalf of his Brother, whose English Name is Thomas McKee; he said that while he was at Fort Augusta he bought a Horse, which Cost him Eighteen Pounds, and he desired Captain Trump to put him into pasture for him amongst the inhabitants; that Captain Trump received the Horses, but kept him in the stable at the

Fort, for the use of the Barracks, where he Contracted a disease of which he dyed, and that he has never been paid for the Horse.

Then Papununk spoke again:

"Brother:

"With regard to what I have mentioned about Religious matters, it may be Some may not think as I do, or may think slightly of these Matters, but I am fixed in my principles, and Shall always abide by them.

"Brother:

"I am glad I have an Opportunity of mentioning these several Matters in the presence of such a large Audience of Young and old Persons. The Great God observes all that passes in our hearts, and hears all that We say to one another."

He then finished with a solemn Act of Prayer and thanksgiving, which he performed very devoutly.

Job Chillaway told Mr. Post privately, that he lent a Portmanteau[4] to Lieutenant Adam Henry, who has lost it, and never paid him for it.

That he was employed to go to Niagara as a spy, for which he does not desire to be paid; but lost an Horse in the Journey, and for it he thinks he should be paid.

---

[4] A valise for traveling.

AT A COUNCIL HELD IN THE STATE HOUSE, ON THURSDAY THE 16TH JULY, 1760.

Present:

The Honourable JAMES HAMILTON, Esqr., Lieutenant Governor.

The Same Members of Council as on the 12th.

A Large Number of the People called Quakers.

The same Indians and Interpreters.

The Governor, addressing himself to Papunuk, spoke as follows:

"Brother:

"We understand you do not come on any Publick business, or to Treat with the Government, and that you were invited by Friends to pay a Religious Visit; And you let us know that you are Lovers of Peace, mindful of the Old friendship, and will always be our Good Friends; This declaration is very agreeable to us; We heartily thank you for it, desire you will persevere in the Same good disposition, and in return, We promise you our sincere Friendship and Assistance on all needful Occasions.

"Brother:

"It gives us great Satisfaction to hear you mention how the Lord has enlightened you. Religion is what all good Men have at heart, and we hope and pray that the day may not be far off when all Mankind as well Indians as others, shall be so enlightened as to hearken to and embrace the Christian Religion, which is so necessary to their everlasting happiness in the world to come.

"Brother:

"You told me that your Young Men would listen to you, and were resolved to regulate their Lives so as to please their Great Creator, and likewise that they would lay aside whatever was bad and displeasing to him. We approve of this just and pious resolution, and heartily rejoice to hear you. It is every Man's Duty to do the same thing, if he will approve himself worthy of the Mercies of the Heavenly Father.

"Brother:

"As to what you have mentioned Concerning our Method of Trading with the Indians We understand you well, and have Communicated what you have said to the Indian Commissioners who are Chose by the Government and People to regulate these Matters; they are present, and they will Confer with you on this subject and settle it to your satisfaction.

"Brother:

"Our presents are small and not offer'd you as a Reward, they are of too little Value to produce the bad Consequences you apprehend.

"We Consider that tho' you come well Cover'd to us, yet the bryers may tear your Stockings, Shirts and Blankets before you reach home, and that you will Want others to appear in when you return to your own People, and would have you therefore accept them, being offer'd to you out of pure love and regard for your welfare.

"Brother:

"As you told us you did not come down on publick Business or to treat with the Government, I have nothing further to say to you at present, But to assure you that your Visit has been very agreeable to me and all the good people of the province, in whose behalf as well as my own, I salute you and wish you a safe and prosperous Journey to your own Habitations. And I pray God Almighty to have you in his holy keeping, and to strengthen more and more the Good Work already begun in your hearts, and make you the happy Instruments of spreading the Same Good and pious disposition among all the Indians."[5]

---

[5] An abridged version of Papoonan's statements at this Council appears in Thomson (1760:1-9). Thomson's account continues as follows:

> It appears that there has been an immediate awakening amongst some of these Indians, more especially of late, when Papoonahoal, who is now their chief, apprehended himself called to preach to them, in which service he was, sometime after joined by two or three more. They appear very earnest in promoting true pity which they apprehend is an inward work by which the heart is changed from bad to good, wch. they express by the heart's becoming soft, & being filled wth good. In this disposition they absolutely refused to join the other Indians in the prosecution of the war; letting them know they would not join in it- tho' they should kill or make Slaves or (as they express it) negroes of them. And I understood that their chief declar'd that whatever argument might be used in defence of the war he was fully perswaded that when God made men he never intended they should kill or destroy one another- Friends had several solid opportunities with them. They regularly attended our Meetings during their stay in town. Keep themselves quite free from Drink and behaved soberly and orderly after expressing their satisfaction with what they had heard from Friends, which they sd. Exactly answered to their own religions prospect, they returned home & were accompanied as far as Bethlehem by a Friend who made some further observations upon their conversation and Conduct on the way and is as follows:
>
> The Behaviour of these Indians in general was commendable, but particularly the behaviour of Papoonahoal their chief, which afforded me some satisfaction as well as a great deal of instruction, for his deportment was such as manifested his mind to be quiet & easie, accompanied with a becoming solidity and gravity. He dropped several expressions which, as they were interpreted to me, appeared worthy of note. Being asked what he thought of war, he answered, "It has been told to my heart that man was not made for that end, therefore I have ceased

from war: yet I have not laboured to bring about a peace so much as I ought to have done. I was made weak for that and by the bad Spirit's striving to overcome the good in my heart, but I hope the good Spirit will overcome the bad and then I shall labour heartily to bring about a peace. I have often thought it strange that the Christians are such great warriours; & I have wondered they are not greater lovers of Peace, for, said he, from the time God first shewed himself to my mind, & put his goodness in my heart, I found myself in such a temper that I thought if the flesh had been whipt off me wth horsewhips I could have borne it without being angry at those that did it.

As we were riding upon the way I had a mind to say something to him concerning our Saviour's words and good examples when on earth. I desired the Interpreter to ask him if he was disposed to hear such things, he answered "Such words are very good and would be very acceptable at a fit time. Such things are awful, and should be spoke of at a Solemn time for then the heart is soft, & they go into it & not be lost but when the heart is hard they will not go into it but fall off from the heart & so are lost, and such words should not be lost. But at a fit time I would be glad to hear these things.

Concerning People reasoning about religion, he said, "When people speak of these things they are apt to stand up in opposition one against the other, as tho' they strove to throw each other down or to see wch is the wisest. Now these things should not be, but whilst one is speacking the other should hold his head down till the first has done, and then speak without being in a heat or angry."

I asked him what he thought was the cause of the altercations of the times, and why they were so changed from what they had been some years past. He answered, "People are grown cross at each other. If they live in love it would not be so, but they grow proud & covetous, which causes God to be angry & send dry & hot Summers & hard winters, & also sickness amongst the people which he would not do if they loved one another and would do as he would have them."

Being at the Indian town, near Bethlehem & setting in company with two or three persons which were conversing on religious matters, he said, "I am apprehensive that I have a feeling sense in my own heart, whereby I know when people speak from the head, or when they speak from ye heart."

I told him many of my friends as well as my self had been thoughtful about the Indians last winter, & had desires for their welfare, & that my heart was made to love many of them tho' I had never seen them. He replied, "I believe this love is of God, for tho' you did not know [ ] should come down, nor we ourselves did not know it, yet God did, therefore he inclined your heart towards us, that you might be the more glad & make us the more welcome when we did come."

I understood by the Interpreter that this Indian no sooner felt the power of God on his heart to his comfort but he endeavoured to make the other Indians sensible of the same & laboured to turn their minds to a search after what he himself had so happily found. One of those Indians who after some time joined him in this work was at first approved of by Papoonahoal, but shewing an inclination to fall back to some of his old corrupt ways, Papoonahoal desired him to be silent, for, says he, "You will spoil the People by speaking from a bad heart.

Go get your own heart made clean first and then come and speak to the People."

The Interpreter gave me an account of the manner in which Papoonahoal was first enlightened which was as follows. "He was formerly a Drunken man, but the death of his father, bringing sorrow over his mind, he fell into a thoughtful melancholly state, in which state his eyes were turned to behold the earth & to consider things that are thereon, & seeing the folly & wickedness that prevailed, his sorrow increased, and it was given to him to believe there was a great power that had created all these things; and his mind was turned from beholding this lower world to look towards him that had created it, and strong desires were begot in his heart for further knowledge of his Creator, nevertheless the Almighty was not yet pleased to be found of him. But his desires increasing he forsook the town and went to the woods in great bitterness of spirit. The other Indians missing him and fearing evil had befallen him, went from the town in search of him, but could not find him; but at the end of five days it pleased God to appear to him to his comfort, and to give him a sight not only of his own inward state, but also an acquaintance into the works of Nature. He also apprehended a sense was given him of the virtues and nature of several herbs, roots, plants, and trees, & the different relation they had to one another; & he was made sensible that man stood in the nearest relation to God of any other part of the Creation. It was at this time he was made sensible of his duty to God, and he came home rejoicing & endeavoured to put in practice what he apprehended what was required of him.

The morning I parted wth them at Bethlehem I told them I intended to set my face homeward, and if any of you have a word of advice to give me I shall hear it gladly. After some pause Papoonahoal spoke as follows.

"Brother, it discovers a good disposition in you to love to hear good council. There are some people that set light by what I say, & will not hear me. Since I first had desires after God People of different notions about religion have spoke to me, all directing me to their particular way, but there is but one way to the place of happiness which God has prepared for his creature man. Brother there are none that ever spoke such good words to me as I have heard from the Quakers; for what they say answers exactly to what has been told my heart before I saw them. When I left home I resolved not to speak to the Quakers but hearken & hear what they would speak to me. I have heard a voice speak to my heart and say, 'The Quakers are right.' It may be a wrong voice, but I believe it is the true voice. However, if the goodness wch I feel in my heart remain wth me I shall come again to see the Quakers, & if I continue to grow strong I hope the time will come that I shall be joined in close fellowship with them."

Since the foregoing account, Papoonahoal the Indian chief, in conversation said, That he thought the Quakers walked the nearest to what Jesus Christ had required of us to do, & that he though war was unlawful. When some in company argued very strongly for a defensive war, and asserting that if a man was to come and kill any of them when it was in their power to prevent it they should be accountable for their own death, the old man answered, That he understood the white people had a book which God had ordered to be wrote for them, wherein they were to be informed that God had made the world, and that he had sent his

MEMORANDUM.

Mr. Frederick Post and Mr. John Hays, who were appointed to Attend Teedyuscung, along with Isaac Stille and Moses Tallamy, to the Great Indian Council to be held by the Western Indians over the Ohio, returned the 1ˢᵗ of this Instant to Bethlehem, having been denied a passage thro' the Seneca Country. Each of them deliver'd the Journal of their Travels and Proceedings, which are ordered to be lodged with the Council Papers.

AT A CONFERENCE WITH THE INDIANS IN THE STATE HOUSE, THURSDAY 14ᵀᴴ AUGUST, 1760.

Present:

The Honourable JAMES HAMILTON, Esquire, Lieutenant Governor.
    Richard Peters, Esquire.
    Robert White,
    John White,
    George White,
    William James,
    Abraham Siscoe,
    Jacob Sinoscoe, Nantycokes.
    Robert Andom,
    Mansieus,
    Manasee, Conoys.

Robert White, after making an Apology for his bad English, addressed the Governor as follows:
"Brother:

"We are of your Brethren, the Nantycokes and Conoys, who live at Chenango, on the upper Waters of sasquehannah. We are not Chiefs, nor are we come on any great Matter of Business. Many of our principal Men are gone with Sir William Johnson to War, and We come to pay our Brethren at Philadelphia a friendly visit.
"Brother:

"I clean your Eyes that you may see me as clearly as at the first. I put my

---

son Jesus Christ into the world to shew us how we shd live. To this it was replied, That this was true. "Well then," said Papoonahoal, "why did not Jesus Christ fight when the people took him to kill him." He also added that he believed the white people were very wicked as they had so great an advantage of that book and lived so contrary to it.

hand unto your throat and pull out every thing that sticks there that might hinder you from speaking. I likewise clear your heart, that there may be a free passage from it. This being the old place where the Council Fire has always Burned, I clear the Floor, Seats, and every thing in the Council Chamber, that you may sit as clean and easy as before. I remember all the Clouds that for some time past have hindred us from seeing the Sun. I pray God may help us all to dispel these quite, that the Sun may Shine as bright as ever.

A String.

"Brother:

"We come to acquaint you that we have a good disposition for peace. Our Grand Fathers always lived in Love and Friendship with the English. They are dead; they were wise people. We are not indeed so wise as they, but We have very good hearts towards our Brethren, and desire to follow the Good Example of our Grand fathers, in living on the same good terms, and with the same friendliness with you as they did. And in token hereof, We do By this Belt clear the road from the Place where we live at Chenango, to this City. We remove out of it all sorts of nastiness. We will not leave any bad or wickedness in it, that both you and we may travel in it with the utmost safety. We are very sincere in what We now say, and speak from our hearts; and We include herein all the people Who live with us, as well the Six Nations as other Indians; they are all heartily desirous that the road may be made perfectly clear."

A Belt.

"Brother:

"There have been some Indians here before us, who live nearer you than We, at a place called Waghaloosen; We heard they had been here, but did not hear what they said to you. We have been under a good deal of Concern on their Account, for these two or three Years; We are right glad they came to you of themselves, and We hope they have spoken good Words to you."

A String.

"What little we had to say is now finished, and tomorrow morning We think of going home again."

After some pause, Robert White arose and spoke again.

"Brother:

"Where we live is a poor place, We have hardly anything to eat or drink, And the Town, thro' which we pass to come here, are as poor as We; It is true they have a supply of Flour from Shamoken, but it is so little that they can allow us Nothing out of it; We desire our Brethren will consider our Circumstance, and give us something to take home with us as well as to subsist on upon the Road."

Robert White acquainted the Governor that one Jno. Ryal now present came to their Town a Year ago along with a German, one Samuel Loots, and told them they would live with them if they pleased to receive them; It seems they were two soldiers belonging to the fourth Battallion of Royal Americans in Garrison at Oswego, and they deserted from thence after the action at Niagara.

Robert White added that the other soldier was left behind sick and might be dead by this time. As to Regal, as he was one of their Brethren, they gave him no Encouragement to continue with them, tho' they should be glad of his stay, as he was a Good Man and had been sent of Errands by them, but they left this entirely to the good will of the Governor; Regal might either stay here or return with them to Chenango as the Governor should give directions, but if he returned it would be necessary he should have a Discharge, or he might be taken up and hanged or Shot.

Robert White said they had likewise with them a French prisoner, taken at Niagara, and in the division of Prisoners given to them by Sir William Johnson, and was adopted among them, and belonged to one of the Indians now present.

AT A CONFERENCE WITH THE INDIANS IN THE STATE HOUSE, THE 15TH AUGUST, 1760.

Present:

The Honourable JAMES HAMILTON, Esquire, Lieutenant Governor.

Richard Peters, Esquire.

The same Indians as Yesterday.

The Governor's answer to the speeches delivered yesterday, by the Nantycokes and Conoy Indians:

"Brethren:

"I receive your Visit kindly, and Am Glad to see you. We have had of late many thick, dark Clouds, which have taken away the sight of the Sun and of one another. You have done well in observing the Ceremonies used by your Ancestors on these Occasions, And by this String I clean your Eyes, Throat, and Heart, and Likewise wipe the Council Seats clean, that you may sit easy with your Brethren, and confer with them freely."

Strings.

"Brethren:

"By this Belt I do, in behalf of this Province, and all the Good People in it, clear the road from this City to the place of your Habitation at Chenango. You may rest assured that none of the King's subjects will molest you in the least. You may Use it very safely on all occasions that require your coming or sending to us."

A Belt.

"Brethren:

"The Indians of Waghaloosen came and paid us a very friendly Visit, and spoke good Words to us, and they expressed great satisfaction with our reception of them, when they took their Leave of us to return home.

"Brethren:

"In consideration of what you said yesterday to us, of the difficulty you met in Getting Provisions on the Road, and how scarce everything was in your Towns, I have provided a Small matter for you which we desire you will accept as a testimony of our regard for you."

The Present of Goods.

AT A COUNCIL HELD IN THE STATE HOUSE,
ON MUNDAY THE 15ᵀᴴ SEPTEMBER, 1760.

Present:

The Honourable JAMES HAMILTON, Esquire, Lieutenant Governor.
Richard Peters, Esquire.
Mr. Pemberton,
Mr. Say,
Mr. Warder, and several other Citizens.
Teedyuscung,
his Son Amos,
Moses Tittamy,
Anondounoakom, the Son of the Chief of the Minisinks,
and Six other Delaware Indians, who attended Teedyuscung in his journey
over the Ohio.
Isaac Stille, Interpreter.

Teedyuscung being returned from the Ohio, waited on the Governor
on Saturday to acquaint him that he had performed the Journey he
undertook, and had brought a deal of Good News. The Governor expressed
his satisfaction at seeing him safe returned, and appointed this day to hear
his news.

After the usual salutations, Teedyuscung arose and spoke:
"Brother:

"I have nothing to Say to you of my own at this time; I shall only now
tell you some News; You may remember that I often promised you to give the
hallo thro' all the Indian Nations. I have been a long way back, a great way
indeed, beyond the Allegheny, among my friends there; when I got as far as
the Salt Lick Town, towards the head of Beaver Creek, I stopped there and
sent Messengers to the Chiefs of all the Indians in those parts, desiring them
to come and hold Council; it took three Weeks to collect them together, and
then, having a large Number gathered together, I communicated to them all
that had passed between me and this Government for four years past, at
which they were glad, and declared that this was the first time they had a
right understanding of these Transactions; they said they heard every now
and then, that we were sitting together about Peace, but they were not
acquainted 'till now with the Particulars of our Several Conferences; I
concealed Nothing from them, and when they had heard all they were right
Glad; It gave joy to their very hearts."

A String.

Then holding a Belt in his hand he proceeded:

"Brother:

"This belt came from an Indian Nation, the Kickabouses,[6] who live a great way beyond the Twicktwees;[7] by it they told me that it was the first time they had heard of my making peace with the English; that they were greatly pleased with it, and joined their hands heartily to it, and they would all agree to what their Grandfathers, the Delawares, should Conclude with the English; they likewise desired Me to let the Governor know that tho' they lived a great way off, further than the other Nations, yet they would come with them in the spring, and hold Council at Philadelphia."

A Belt.

"Brother:

"My Son Amos, sitting there, is a Warrior and Captain. I took him along with me, and at this great Meeting of Indians I gave him a Belt to speak to the Warriors, as from me to join in the Peace. So after the old men had done holding the Council the Warriors went by themselves and held a Council together, and agreed as one man to every thing that we had Concluded upon, and would heartily keep the Peace; they had pitied the Old Men, Women, and Children; and 'tho they had hitherto kept their hands shut, yet they would now open them, and no longer keep the English Flesh and Blood within their hands, but open them and set all the prisoners at Liberty."

A String.

"Brother:

"As I went along that part of the Country where the Munsies now live, I took along this young man, pointing to (Anondounoakom). He is the Son of their principal man, and was very willing to go, havg. a desire to hear what should be said on all sides. After the General Council was over, he was mightyly pleased with it, and in order to enable him to relate faithfully all that had passed, and to use his influence, that all his Nation might concur with it, I gave him two Belts and Eight Fathom of Wampum. I had a particular reason for doing so, because I knew their Nation had taken many

---

[6] The Kickapoos, a Central Algonguian-speaking people then living in Illinois.

[7] A confederation of related Algonquian-speaking nations residing in Indiana. The name Twicktwees refers to the alarm call of the crane. This confederation is most widely known as the Miamis.

Prisoners, and that they detained them in their Towns; so I thought this would incline him to get them delivered up."

A Belt.

"Brother:

"You know that we have been sitting together these four Years past. All the Indian Nations back, yea, a great way back, have heard all the particulars that have passed between us. All their Chiefs and all their Warriors have made themselves as one Man, and have formed their hands to our Peace, and promise never to break it, but to hold the Peace Belt fast. The Warriors have agreed to confirm what the Old Men have done. In consequence of this, I assure you no one Nation Shall hereafter quarrel with you or with one another, without its first being determined in a General Indian Council, at which it is agreed that the English shall be present. This is the unanimous determination of all the Indian Nations that I have seen, viz.: the Tarons,[8] the Nelametenos or Owendaots,[9] the Twicktwees,[10] the Shawonese, the Chippaways, all the Tribes of the Delaware and others, to the Number of ten Nations, all principal Nations of those who live far back to the Westward; they have all agreed to what has been said on the Belts and strings, which I have now deliver'd."

A string.

"Brother:

"This is all I have to say at this time. Tomaquior,[11] the Beaver King (who is the head man of the Delawares at the Ohio), did not give me anything in Charge to say to the Governor. We were all present at the great Council held at Pittsburg, and heard him tell the General that he would go to Philadelphia in the Summer, and hold a Council with this Government, in Complyance with the Several Invitations he had received from it. I told Tamaqui that Pittsburgh was only a place for Warriors to speak in, and that he should do no Council Business at Pitsburg. And accordingly Tomaqui told the General that he would not say any thing to him, but say it at the place where their Grand fathers were always used to hold Council with the

---

[8] From Ontarahronon, "lake people," an Iroquoian term for Kickapoo. See ff.5 , p. 137.

[9] Wyandots. See ff. 77, p. 94.

[10] Miamis. See ff. 6, p. 137.

[11] Tamaqua. See ff.,87, p. 100.

English.

"Brother:

"This is all. I think to come and visit you to-Morrow, and to talk over many things that I have seen in my Journey."

The Governor said he would be glad to see him, and in the mean time he would Confer with the provincial Commissioners what had been said, and as soon as he should know their minds he would give him an Answer.

The Governor returned Teedyuscung thanks for his Speeches, and the next day made him a present of Goods, which he thankfully received.

September 17th, 1760; the following Letter, received from Mr. Holland, the Indian Agent at Shamokin, was ordered to be entered:

"SHAMOKIN, 9 Mo. 17th, 1760.

"Permit me to acquaint the Governor:

"That John Hatson arrived here on the 15th, in 8 days, from Margarets Town, and deliver'd me the inclosed String of Wampum, and the following speech, which he said was sent to the Governor by Catharine, the Daughter of French Margaret.

"That She desired, by this String of Wampum, to acquaint the Governor of the receipt of his by Papunohoal, and that she was sorry the indisposition of her Family had so long prevented her from complying with the Governor's request to bring down the Prisoners, but that She would be down this Fall with the two that belonged to her, and desired that She may not be blamed for her Sisters carrying the Woman She has to the Allegany, as it was not in her power to prevail with her to take her to Philadelphia; in Confirmation of which she sent the Governor the inclosed String of Wampum.

"John informed me that Molley was set off for the Allegany with the White Woman after he left the Town, and that he expected Cate here in ten days, and that he should go with her to Philadelphia and deliver them to the Governor.

"From thy friend,

"NATHANIEL HOLLAND."

A CONFERENCE WITH TEEDYUSCUNG,
THE 18TH DAY OF SEPTEMBER, 1760.

Present:

The Honourable JAMES HAMILTON, Esquire, Lieutenant Governor.

Richard Peters, Esquire.

"Brother:

"I am ready to set out, but have heard yesterday some bad news which obliges me once more to wait upon you.

"Yesterday I was told that some of the new England People are gone on the West side of Sasquehannah with intent to Settle the Lands at Wyomink; If this should be the case, then all the pains that have been taken by this Government and me will be to no purpose; It is the Indians Land, and they will not suffer it to be settled, I therefore desire the Governor will send a Smart Letter to the Government where those intruding People came from, to forbid this proceeding, and tell their Governor plainly that if they do not go away the Indians will turn them off; he added, with a great deal of Warmth, these people cannot pretend Ignorance, and if they Shall then continue on the Lands it will be their own fault if any thing happens, and repeated his Entreaties to the Governor to take every measure in his power to prevent the settlement of those Lands, for it will certainly bring on another Indian war."

The Governor informed Teedyuscung that he had the other day received Some information on this Matter, and that as the Justices of the peace were holding a Court at Easton, he ordered the Sheriff and some of the said Justices to go to the place where it is said these New England people are settling, and if they find any people settling to let them know they are sent by this Government to warn them of, and show them the bad Consequences that would ensue on such an Encroachment on Lands belonging to the Indians and the Proprietaries, and forthwith to report what they find doing, that proper measures may be taken to prevent it.

Teedyuscung further desired that he might be made acquainted with whatever is doing of this sort, for if the Governor can't the Indians will put a Stop to it, and he was answered that he should certainly be informed of it.

ASSOCIATED DOCUMENTS: AFTERMATH

AT A CONFERENCE WITH TEEDYUSCUNG
ON THE 13TH DAY OF NOVEMBER, 1760

Present:

The Honourable JAMES HAMILTON, Esquire, Lieutenant Governor.
Richard Peters, Esquire.

Teedyuscung waited on the Governor and produced a Letter from Sir William Johnson to him, dated Fort Johnson, 1ˢᵗ March, 1760,[12] in these words:

"Fort Johnson, March 1ˢᵗ, 1760.

"Brother Teedyuscung:

"His Majesty, King George, having, in consequence of what passed at the Conferences in July and August, 1757, at Easton, taken into Consideration your Complaint, then made, Concerning Lands which you alledge you have been deprived of without your consent, or satisfaction made you for the same, and out of his Great Goodness and regard for Justice, which he is remarkable for, as well as his Love for his Children, the Indians, has ordered me to examine thoroughly into the said Affair, and when I have made a full and particular Enquiry into the Circumstances of the case, and hear what all partys may he to offer, to transmit to him my proceedings in that Business.

"In obedience, therefore, to his Majesty's Command, I do now take the earliest opportunity by your Son, who is the Bearer of this, acquainting you with his pleasure, and I desire to know when a Meeting with you and such Delawares or others as are concerned in the affair may be had for that purpose; also where it may be most convenient for you and them to meet me. The sooner I know this the better, that I may give notice to the Proprietaries' Commissioners to attend, and that it may not interfere with my Military Duty the ensuing Campaign, in which I hope and expect you and your Nation will, in return for his Majesty's Kind Intentions towards you, be ready to act a Brother-like part against his enemies when called upon.

"I am your well-wisher and Sincere Brother
"WILLIAM JOHNSON.

"To Teedyuscung, Chief of the Delawares."

He told the Governor that this letter was brought to him by his son, just as he was setting out for Citsintsing,[13] and in an Angry kind of a Tone, said he would have nothing to do with Sir William Johnson; he did not incline

---

[12] Copies of this letter are also published in O'Callaghan (1849-52[2]: 789-90) and Sullivan et al (1921-65 [3]: 194-95).

[13] Assinisink.

that the matter should be heard by him, but desired it might be heard by the Governor. The Governor made answer that it was referred to Sir William Johnson by the King, on his petition preferr'd to his Majesty by the Assembly. Teedyuscung replied, that he knew it to be so, but for all that he should not chuse Sir William Johnson should have any thing to do with it, and repeated his request to the Governor to hear it himself; to which the Governor made Answer, that sine this was his request, and he was so very earnest in it, he would take it into Consideration; but then as he was informed, that the Lands about which the Complaint was made, did belong formerly to distant Indians, some living on the Susquehannah, and others to the Westward of the Ohio, he did insist with Teedyuscung that all these Indians should be informed of, and agree to his proposal, and attend the Treaty. Teedyuscung replied, that this was right, and assured the Governor that this Matter had been talked of at the Ohio, with Chingas and other Indians who were interested in these Lands, who thought as he did, and promised to be at Philadelphia in the spring.

After a Short pause, he took some Wampum out of his Pocket, consisting of Four strings, two White and two Black.

And then acquainted the Governor that the White part was sent from Secaughceeny, to inform him that a party of Indians came there to Council, and produced in Council a Belt from the French, desiring their Assistance against the English, who had beat them, but they declined to have any thing to do with it, and sent the French Belt forward to Teedyuscung, and thereupon he came down to inform the Governor about it; he added that the Governor was his Ear in Philadelphia, and he was the Governor's Ear in Wyomink, and it was all one as if the Governor himself was there.

A String.

Teedyuscung enquired earnestly of the Governor what he had done about the settlement of the New England People that he had informed him of the last time he was in Town. The Governor acquainted him that the Sheriff and Magistrates of Northampton County were returned from Cushatunk[14] and had made their report to him that they found about Twenty families from Connicticut there, who said they had good Deeds from some Jersey Delaware Indians for those Lands, and would settle them, but he would not suffer it, and take the best measures in his power to have them removed. Teedyuscung replied, that the Indians were very uneasy, and would certainly turn them away if he would not; as to Deeds from Jersey Indians, that must be a pretence; those Indians would not give deeds.

---

[14] Present-day Damascus, Pennsylvania, on the western banks of the upper Delaware River.

REFERENCES

BECKER, MARSHALL J.
1992   Teedyuscung's Youth and Hereditary Land Rights in New
    Jersey: The Identification of the Unalachtigo. *Bulletin of*
    the Archaeological Society of New Jersey 47:37-60.

CHASE. THOMAS C.
1980   Christian Frederick Post, 1715-1785: Missionary and
    Diplomat to the Indians of America. Unpublished Ed.D.
    dissertation, Department of Education, Pennsylvania
    State University, State College.

DONEHOO, GEORGE P.
1928   *Indian Villages and Place Names in Pennsylvania.* Harrisburg:
    The Telegraph Press.

DOWD, GREGORY EVANS
1992   *A Spirited Resistance: The North American Indian Struggle for*
    Unity, 1745-1815. Baltimore: The Johns Hopkins Press.

EDMUNDS, R. DAVID, and JOSEPH L. PEYSER
1993   *The Fox Wars: The Mesquakie Challenge to New France.*
    Norman: University of Oklahoma Press.

FLEXNER, JOHN THOMAS
1979   *Mohawk Baronet: A Biography of Sir William Johnson.*
    Revised edition. Syracuse: Syracuse University Press.

GRUMET, ROBERT S.
1995   *Historic Contact: Indian People and Colonists in Today's*
    Northeastern United States in the Sixteenth through Eighteenth
    Centuries. Norman: University of Oklahoma Press

HAMILTON, MILTON W.
1976   *Sir William Johnson, Colonial American, 1715-1763.* Port
    Washington, New York: Kennikat Press.

HAUPTMAN, LAURENCE M.
1980   Refugee Havens: The Iroquois Villages of the Eighteenth
               Century. In Christopher Vecsey and Robert Venables,
               editors, *American Indian Environments: Ecological Issues in
               Native American History*, pp. 128-39. Syracuse: Syracuse
               University Press.

HAZARD, SAMUEL, editor
1852a   *Minutes of the Provincial Council of Pennsylvania, from the
               Organization to the Termination of the Proprietary Govern-
               ment*, 10 vols. Harrisburg.
1852b   *Pennsylvania Archives*. 1ˢᵗ Series. 12 vols. Harrisburg.

HULBERT, ARCHER BUTLER, and WILLIAM NATHANIEL SCHWARZE,
               editors
1912   The Diaries of Zeisberger Relating to the First Mission in
               the Ohio Basin. *Ohio Archaeological and Historical
               Quarterly* 21:1-125.

HUNTER, WILLIAM A.
1954   (editor) John Hays' Diary and Journal of 1760. *Pennsyl-
               vania Archaeologist* 24(2):63-84.
1960   *Forts of the Pennsylvania Frontier, 1753-58*. Harrisburg:
               Pennsylvania Museum and Historical Commission.
1981   (editor) *Indians in Pennsylvania*. By Paul A. W. Wallace.
               Revised Edition. Harrisburg: Pennsylvania Museum and
               Historical Commission.
1996   Moses (Tunda) Tatamy, Delaware Indian Diplomat. In
               Robert S. Grumet, editor, *Northeastern Indian Lives, 1632-
               1816*, pp. 258-71. Amherst: University of Massachusetts
               Press [Reprint of the original article first published in
               Herbert C. Kraft, editor, *A Delaware Indian Symposium*
               (1974). Harrisburg: Pennsylvania Museum and Historical
               Commission.]

JENNINGS, FRANCIS
1976   *The Invasion of America: Indians, Colonialism, and the Cant
               of Conquest*. New York: W. W. Norton.

REFERENCES

1984 *The Ambiguous Iroquois Empire: The Covenant Chain Confederation of Indian Tribes with English Colonies from its Beginnings to the Lancaster Treaty of 1744.* New York: W. W. Norton.

1988 *Empire of Fortune: Crowns, Colonies, and Tribes in the Seven Years War in America.* New York: W. W. Norton.

JONES, DOROTHY V.
1982 *License for Empire: Colonization by Treaty in Early America.* Chicago: University of Chicago Press.

KENT, BARRY C.
1984 *Susquehanna's Indians.* Anthropological Series No. 6. Harrisburg: Pennsylvania Historical and Museum Commission.

MANCALL, PETER C.
1991 *Valley of Opportunity: Economic Culture along the Upper Susquehanna, 1700-1800.* Ithaca: Cornell University Press.

MCCONNELL, MICHAEL N.
1992 A Country Between: *The Upper Ohio Valley and its Peoples, 1724-1774.* Lincoln: University of Nebraska Press.

1996 Pisquetomen and Tamaqua: Mediating Peace in the Ohio Country. In Robert S. Grumet, editor, *Northeastern Indian Lives, 1632-1816,* pp. 273-94. Amherst: University of Massachusetts Press.

MACKINNEY, GERTRUDE, and CHARLES F. HOBAN, editors
1931-35 Votes and Proceedings of the House of Representatives of the Province of Pennsylvania [1752-76]. *Pennsylvania Archives,* 8th ser., 8 vols. Harrisburg.

MERRELL, JAMES H.
1999 *Into the American Woods: Negotiators on the Pennsylvania Frontier.* New York: W.W. Norton.

O'CALLAGHAN, EDMUND BURKE, editor
1849-51   *Documentary History of the State of New York.* 4 vols.
Albany: Weed, Parsons.

O'CALLAGHAN, EDMUND BURKE, and BERTHOLD FERNOW, editors
1853-87   *Documents Relative to the Colonial History of the State of New York.* 15 vols, Albany: Weed, Parsons.

POST, CHRISTIAN FREDERICK
1760   Journal of Christian Frederick Post, April 1, 1760-June 30, 1760. Contemporary copy of Post's Indian mission. Attending Teedyuscung toward the Ohio, Post and Hays were denied passage through the Seneca country and obliged to return to Bethlehem. Gift of the Friends Historical Association, January 17, 1949. (Am 12605) Manuscript on file, Historical Society of Pennsylvania. Philadelphia.

1904   Two Journals of Western Tours [1758-59]. In Rueben Gold Thwaites, editor, *Early Western Journals, 1748-1765,* pp. 177-291. Cleveland: The Arthur H. Clark Company.

STEVENS, S. K., et al., editors
1972-94   *The Papers of Henry Bouquet.* 6 vols. Harrisburg: Pennsylvania Museum and Historical Commission.

SULLIVAN, JAMES, ALEXANDER C. FLICK, ALMON W. LAUBER, MILTON W. HAMILTON, and ALBERT B. COREY, editors
1921-65   *The Papers of Sir William Johnson.* 15 vols. Albany: The State University of New York.

TANNER, HELEN HORNBECK
1987   *Atlas of Great Lakes Indian History.* Norman: University of Oklahoma Press.

THOMSON, CHARLES
1760   *Some Account of the Behaviour & Sentiments of a Number of Well-disposed Indians Mostly of the Minusing-Tribe.*

REFERENCES

Manuscript on file, Miscellaneous Manuscripts, Friends
Historical Society, Haverford, Pennsylvania.

VAUGHAN, ALDEN T.
1984   Frontier Banditti and the Indians: The Paxton Boys'
               Legacy, 1763-1775. *Pennsylvania History* 51(1):1-29.

WALLACE, ANTHONY F. C.
1990   *King of the Delawares: Teedyuscung, 1700-1763.* Syracuse:
               Syracuse University Press [Reprint of the 1949 edition
               first published by the University of Pennsylvania Press].

WALLACE, PAUL A. W.
1965   *Indian Paths of Pennsylvania.* Harrisburg: Pennsylvania
               Museum and Historical Commission.

WHITE, RICHARD
1991   *The Middle Ground: Indians, Empires, and Republics in the
               Great Lakes Region, 1650-1815.* New York: Cambridge
               University Press.

INDEX

INDEX

INDEX